NEWFOUNDL

Knits for Little Ones

15 original patterns
designed for children

KATIE NOSEWORTHY

For Philip

Library and Archives Canada Cataloguing in Publication
Title: Newfoundland knits for little ones : 15 original patterns designed for children /
Katie Noseworthy.
Names: Noseworthy, Katie, author.
Description: Includes bibliographical references.
Identifiers: Canadiana 20220200599 | ISBN 9781989417645
Subjects: LCSH: Knitting—Newfoundland and Labrador—Patterns. |
LCSH: Children's clothing—Newfoundland and Labrador. |
LCSH: Knitwear—Newfoundland and Labrador. | LCGFT: Pattern books.
Classification: LCC TT819.C32 N496 2023 | DDC 746.43/2043209718—dc23

© 2023 Katie Noseworthy

Published by Boulder Books
Portugal Cove-St. Philip's, Newfoundland and Labrador
www.boulderbooks.ca

Design and layout: Tanya Montini
Editor: Stephanie Porter
Copy editor: Iona Bulgin

Printed in China

We acknowledge the financial support of the Government of Newfoundland and Labrador
through the Department of Tourism, Culture, Arts and Recreation.

Funded by the Government of Canada
Financé par le gouvernement du Canada

Canada

NEWFOUNDLAND
Knits for Little Ones

**15 original patterns
designed for children**

BOULDER
BOOKS

KATIE NOSEWORTHY

Contents

Patterns

Introduction

I have always been a maker—obsessed with craft projects and art supplies, baking, writing, anything that would let me put things together. So it surprised absolutely no one that I took to knitting like the proverbial moth to the flame. In 2017, after knitting for about 10 years, I decided to try my hand at putting my ideas on paper and out into the world as a knitwear designer. My life was about finding time to knit.

Then, in 2020, I became a mom. Suddenly, knitting wasn't the most important part of my day. I traded needles for diapers, luxury merino yarn for flannel burp cloths, thumbing through knitting books for frantically searching Dr. Google to understand my kid's latest quirk. Like many women before me, I lost myself to motherhood. I was still knitting, just not as feverishly. Eventually, the haze of new motherhood began to lift and, with it, returned my desire to be someone other than "mom." This collection represents the bridging of both my worlds.

Creating this book also allowed me to explore my sense of place and what that means for me creatively. Knitting is part of our Newfoundland and Labrador identity. Everyone had a basket of handknit mitts and socks for playing outside in the snow. Everyone had a scratchy handknit sweater they were forced to wear. And everyone has skated across their nan's floors in a pair of knit slippers at least once in their lifetime. Newfoundland knitting—while full of artistry and skill—was a functional part of life, whether you liked it or not. And I now understand the value in having long-lasting garments that could stretch and be worn in three out of the four seasons.

When I was approached about putting together a Newfoundland and Labrador kids' collection, I couldn't imagine a better way to honour my new family and my connection to my home. This collection is a tribute to our knitting tradition, inspired by the garments and styles worn by kids throughout our history, and designed to create beautiful and functional knitwear for today's kids. It has been a labour of love and pride and I am so glad that I get to share it with you. I sincerely hope you enjoy it and that it leads to many hours of happy knitting, play, and memories.

knitting for Kids

There's no denying that knitwear comes with certain stigmas—we've all been the victim of a too small, too itchy sweater as a kid. But with updated designs and yarns, knitwear and accessories still have a place in kids' wardrobes. Here are some things we knitters can do to make kids actually want to wear and use what we make for them.

When in doubt, size up

Kids need to be able to move, so being restricted in any way is not going to work. If you're unsure of the best size, you're better off going up a size to give them room to play and room to grow.

Opt for wide necks

The neck is one of the more sensitive areas when it comes to the prickle of yarn. No matter what material you're using, having a tight-fitted neck is bound to be uncomfortable. Try to find patterns that have a wider or boat-style neck.

Be mindful of yarn weight

A baby in a chunky cabled sweater may look adorable, but if the material is too heavy or bulky, they will be weighed down and miserable. Light- to medium-weight yarns will be more comfortable options for babies and toddlers.

Follow safety best practices

We never want our knitwear to become hazards. For older kids, this isn't as much of a worry as it is for babies and toddlers. Make sure that all ends are woven in to avoid getting wrapped around little fingers and toes. Omit decorative buttons and attachments, as these are a choking hazard. Remember that blankets are for supervised sleep and cuddles only.

Stick with the basics

I have a vivid memory of my brother being given a dinosaur sweater that everyone thought was adorable. But at the age of 4, he was absolutely mortified by it. So, unless it's specifically requested by the kid, you're better off sticking with the basics. Well-made basics pair well with everyday clothing, will last through kids' various interests, and can be passed down to family or friends regardless of gender or interests.

Get the kids involved!

Get kids to pick the pattern or colours; take them yarn shopping or anything that allows them to choose what they wear. Kids know what they like and dislike, so letting them have a say will increase the chances that an item is actually worn or used. For babies and toddlers, talk to the parents to get their input.

spinning yarns

A chat about picking the best yarn for your project

Let's be honest: the best part about knitting is the yarn shopping. And these days we are fortunate to have a variety of options available to us. The tricky part is that it can be overwhelming to narrow down which yarns are best for your project and for the intended wearer.

Don't count out wool

Wool is amazing—it's natural, warm, and sustainable. But it has gotten a bad rap for being too high maintenance and too prickly for kids. However, the wool industry has come a long way. Now it's possible to find soft, durable wool and fair price points. And the growing availability of superwash yarns means that the finished item can withstand more frequent washing and even go in a machine.

Test the "prickle factor"

No matter if you're going with natural or synthetic fibres, most kids will still prefer softer yarns. Their skin is much more sensitive to the prickle of yarn than adults'. In fact, what is often mistaken for a wool allergy is actually just irritation. An easy way to test for prickles is to hold the yarn to your neck and under the chin. That isn't to say that there aren't kids who wear more rustic style yarns, because there certainly are. But unless you know that about the kid who will be wearing the item, you're better off erring on the side of softness.

Consider the maintenance

Whatever you're making, consider the person who will be responsible for cleaning it, especially if it's being given as a gift. Sometimes reaching out to the giftee to see what they would prefer is the safest bet. Some people are okay with handwashing, others are not. If you do decide to go with a natural fibre that needs a little extra care, it's never a bad idea to include a "care card" with instructions on how to keep the item in its best condition.

Don't blow your budget (unless you want to!)

The best part of knitting being more popular is that it has led to a larger price range for yarns. There are synthetic yarns and blends for which you can sometimes even get a coupon, extra-bougie hand-dyed one-of-a-kind skeins, and everything in between. Great online-only retailers have high-quality yarns at every price point, and most local yarn stores also try to provide the same to appeal to a broader customer base. Sometimes, you can even luck into someone destashing their yarn for a steal! This makes it so much easier for knitting and knitwear to be accessible, no matter the budget.

No Such Thing as Bad Weather

If the province of Newfoundland and Labrador is known for anything (aside from puffins and icebergs), it's our weather. The summers are short, the winters are long, and rain, drizzle, and fog are typical all year round. But despite all that, the people who live here are very attached to outdoor life: hiking and camping, hunting and gathering, and sometimes just for a quick boil-up. If we waited for the perfect day, we'd never do anything.

When a day can go from freezing in the morning to blistering hot by lunch, knowing how to dress your kid requires a crystal ball.

Ultimately, we want to make it as easy as possible for our kids to get outside and play. Time outside is associated with better physical and mental health, better emotional regulation, and even better ability to focus. Best of all, outside play doesn't need to be structured. Simply allowing kids to explore, dig in the dirt, attempt to climb trees, and pick flowers *is* playing. The best thing we can do for little brains is to give them the opportunity and space to explore outside. I've found wool and knit garments to be a great solution: easy to layer, has natural stretch, and can be worn across seasons. Most importantly, knit garments are much easier to play in than big, puffy coats, and usually just as warm. They still protect from the elements, but give kids a more enjoyable experience.

OUTDOOR SCAVENGER HUNT

Want to get outside but not sure where to go or what to do? Find your favourite outdoor space (a backyard, a park, a trail, etc.) and challenge your kids to hunt for outdoor treasures!

1. A snail
2. The perfect leaf
3. A Y-shaped stick
4. Something fuzzy
5. A yellow flower
6. Three types of birds
7. Something edible
8. A spiderweb
9. A fun-shaped cloud
10. A feather
11. Something pointy
12. A flat rock
13. A puddle
14. A footprint
15. Something round

saltbox A pair of slipper socks

Keep little toes warm with these slippers modelled after the classic hunting sock. The folded cuff keeps the slipper on the foot while kids walk, run, and skate across the floor. The slipper is first knit flat and then joined to work in the round for the toe. The cuff stitches are picked up and worked in the round and then folded over, with options to add buttons for embellishment.

SKILL LEVEL
Experienced beginner

Skills required:
knitting flat, knitting in the round, ribbing, decreasing, picking up stitches, colour changing

MATERIALS
Approximately 90 (100, 110, 121, 133, 146) yds / 82 (91, 101, 111, 122, 134) m worsted weight yarn; 36 (40, 44, 48, 53, 59) yds / 33 (37, 40, 44, 49, 54) m for Foot, 45 (50, 55, 61, 67, 73) yds / 41 (46, 50, 56, 61, 67) m for Cuff MC, and 9 (10, 11, 12, 13, 15) yds / 8 (9, 10, 11, 12, 14) m for Cuff CC. Sample shown in Lion Brand Wool Ease Nightshade, Natural, and Tawny Port, 197 yds / 180 m per 85 g ball.

4.0 mm (US 6) needles for knitting flat and in the round
4.5 mm (US 7) needles for knitting flat and in the round
Or size required to obtain gauge

Tapestry needle

GAUGE
22 sts and 28 rnds = 4" / 10 cm, in stockinette stitch with 4.0 mm (US 6) needles

SIZES
Baby (Toddler, Child, Adult Small, Adult Medium, Adult Large)
Finished foot circumference: 4.5 (5, 5.5, 6, 6.5, 7.5)" / 11 (13, 14, 15, 17, 19) cm
Designed to be worn with negative ease

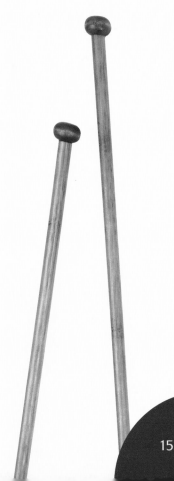

INSTRUCTIONS

Foot

With 4.0 mm (US 6) needles and yarn for the foot, CO 24 (26, 30, 34, 38, 42) sts.

Row 1 (RS): [K1, P1] 3 (3, 4, 4, 5, 5) times, K12 (14, 14, 18, 18, 22), [P1, K1] 3 (3, 4, 4, 5, 5) times.
Row 2 (WS): [P1, K1] 3 (3, 4, 4, 5, 5) times, P12 (14, 14, 18, 18, 22), [K1, P1] 3 (3, 4, 4, 5, 5) times.

Rep rows 1 and 2 until the piece measures 2.5 (3, 3.75, 4.5, 5, 5.5)" / 6.5 (7.5, 9.5, 11.5, 12.5, 14) cm from the CO edge, ending after a WS row.

Next Row: [K1, P1] 3 (3, 4, 4, 5, 5) times, K12 (14, 14, 18, 18, 22), [P1, K1] 3 (3, 4, 4, 5, 5) times, CO 1, join to work in the rnd. 25 (27, 31, 35, 39, 43) sts.

Rnd 1: [K1, P1] 3 (3, 4, 4, 5, 5) times, K12 (14, 14, 18, 18, 22), [P1, K1] 3 (3, 4, 4, 5, 5) times, P1.

Rep rows 1 until the piece measures approximately 4 (5, 6.5, 8, 9, 10.5)" / 10 (12.5, 16.5, 20.5, 23, 26.5) cm, or 0.5" / 1.5 cm shorter than desired length.

Dec Rnd 1: K1, *K2tog; rep from * to end. 13 (14, 16, 18, 20, 22) sts rem.
Next Rnd: Work even.
Dec Rnd 2: K1 (0, 0, 0, 0, 0), *K2tog; rep from * to end. 7 (7, 8, 9, 10, 11) sts rem.

Cut yarn, leaving a 6" / 15 cm tail. Thread tail through sts and pull tightly to close. Weave in end on WS. Seam heel by stitching a "T" seam: Seam vertically (starting with sts toward the sole about two-thirds of the way down.

Next push the remaining edges together horizontally (the sole stitches will be connecting with the remaining sts). Weave in all ends.

Cuff

Using 4.0 mm (US 6) needles and cuff MC, start at the back of the heel with the RS facing and pick up and knit 24 (28, 36, 40, 44, 48) sts. Join to knit in the round.

Work in K1, P1 ribbing for 1.75 (2, 2.25, 2.5, 2.75, 3)" / 4.5 (5, 6, 6.5, 7, 7.5) cm.

Switch to 4.5 mm (US 7) needles.

Increase Rnd: *P6 (7, 9, 10, 11, 12), M1P; rep from * to end of rnd. 28 (32, 40, 44, 48, 52) sts.

Work in K2, P2 ribbing for 1.25 (1.5, 1.75, 1.75, 2, 2.25)" / 3 (4, 4.5, 4.5, 5, 6) cm. Join CC and begin stripes.

Rnd 1: With CC, P to end.
Rnd 2: *K2, P2; rep from * to end of rnd.
Rnd 3: With MC, P to end.
Rnds 4–5: *K2, P2; rep from * to end of rnd.
Rnd 6: With CC, P to end.
Rnd 7: *K2, P2; rep from * to end of rnd.
Rnd 8: With MC, P to end.

Cut CC, leaving a 6" / 15 cm tail. Continue working in K2, P2 ribbing with MC for 0.75 (1, 1.25, 1.5, 1.75, 2)" / 2 (2.5, 3, 4, 4.5, 5) cm. Bind off loosely using the knitted lace bind off (see Special Techniques).

Finishing

Weave in all ends. Fold cuff down so that the RS of the cuff faces outward. Block gently if desired. You may wish to add buttons to the outer side of the cuff as decoration, though this is not recommended for children under the age of 4 as buttons are a choking hazard.

caubvick A pair of colourwork pants

Stretchy, colourful, and warm, these little pants feature colourful designs along the legs using two-colour stranded techniques. Instructions include short row shaping, grow-with-me cuffs and waistbands that give extra time before sizing up and a drawstring waist that keeps the pants in place no matter how much crawling, walking, or running they endure.

SKILL LEVEL
Intermediate

Skills required:
knitting in the round, picking up stitches, eyelets, stranded colourwork, short rows, increasing, decreasing

MATERIALS
Approximately 283 (327, 371, 428, 489, 556, 634) yds / 259 (299, 339, 391, 447, 508, 580) m worsted-weight yarn (see table for breakdown). Shown in Cascade 220 Superwash, 220 yds / 201 m per 100 g ball, col. 1913 "Jet" for MC, assorted worsted-weight yarns for each CC.

	0–6 mo	6–12 mo	1–2 yrs	2–4 yrs	4–6 yrs	6–8 yrs	8–10 yrs
MC	283 yds/259 m	327 yds/299 m	371 yds/339 m	428 yds/391 m	489 yds/447 m	556 yds/509 m	634 yds/680 m
CC (total)	64 yds/59 m	84 yds/77 m	101 yds/92 m	128 yds/117 m	159 yds/145 m	193 yds/177 m	235 yds/215 m
CC1	30 yds/28 m	30 yds/28 m	30 yds/28 m	30 yds/28 m	30 yds/28 m	45yds/41 m	45yds/41 m
CC2	15 yds/14 m	30 yds/28 m	30 yds/28 m	30 yds/28 m	30 yds/28 m	45 yds/41 m	45 yds/41 m
CC3	15 yds/14 m	15 yds/14 m	15 yds/14 m	30 yds/28 m	30 yds/28 m	30 yds/28 m	45 yds/41 m
CC4	15 yds/14 m	15 yds/14 m	15 yds/14 m	15 yds/14 m	30 yds/28 m	30 yds/28 m	30 yds/28 m

4.0 mm (US 6) needles for knitting in the round
4.5 mm (US 7) needles for knitting in the round
Or size required to obtain gauge

Tapestry needle, stitch marker

GAUGE
20.5 sts and 28 rnds = 4" / 10 cm, in stockinette stitch

SIZES
0–6 mo (6–12 mo, 1–2, 2–4, 4–6, 6–8, 8–10)
Finished waist measurements: 18 (18.5, 20, 21, 22, 22.5, 23.5)" / 46 (47, 51, 53, 56, 57, 60) cm
Meant to be worn with 0–1.5" / 0–4 cm of negative ease

INSTRUCTIONS

Waistband

Using 4.0 mm (US 6) needles and MC, CO 92 (96, 104, 108, 112, 120, 132) sts. Join to work in the rnd, being careful not to twist the sts. Place BOR M; this indicates the front of the pants.

Work in K2, P2 ribbing for 8 (8, 10, 10, 10, 12, 12) rnds.

Eyelet Rnd: Work in rib patt for 9 (11, 11, 8, 7, 11, 17) sts, yo, K2tog, *work 7 (7, 8, 7, 6, 6, 6) sts in patt, yo, K2tog; rep from * to last 9 (11, 11, 8, 7, 11, 17) sts, work rem 9 (11, 11, 8, 7, 11, 17) sts in patt.

Work in K2, P2 ribbing for 8 (8, 10, 10, 10, 12, 12) rnds. Repeat Eyelet Rnd.

Work in K2, P2 ribbing for 8 (8, 10, 10, 10, 12, 12) rnds.

Pants

Switch to 4.5 mm (US 7) needles.

Increase Rnd: *K0 (0, 26, 27, 14, 10, 11), M0 (0, 1, 1, 1, 1, 1); rep to end of rnd. 92 (96, 108, 112, 120, 132, 144) sts.

Work in St st for 1.75 (2. 2.25, 2.5, 2.75, 3, 3.5)" / 4 (5, 6, 6.5, 7, 8, 9) cm.

Short Rows

Row 1 (RS): K69 (72, 81, 84, 90, 99, 108), W&T (see Special Techniques).
Row 2 (WS): P46 (48, 54, 56, 60, 66, 72), W&T.
Row 3: K to 4s sts before wrapped stitch, W&T.
Row 4: P to 4s sts before wrapped stitch, W&T.
Work Rows 3–4 a total of 4 (4, 5, 5, 5, 6, 6) times. You should have 6 (8, 4, 6, 10, 6, 12) unworked sts left at the centre.

Pick Up Rnd: K to BOR M, picking up wrapped sts as you go and knitting them together with the sts, Sl M, continue knitting in the rnd, picking up the remaining wrapped stitches and knitting them together with the stitches, K to BOR M.

Work in St st until the front measures 4 (3.5, 4, 3.5, 3.5, 4.25, 5)" / 10 (9, 10, 9, 9, 11, 13) cm from the beginning of the St st section.

Increase Rnd: K1, M1L, K to last 3 sts, M1R, K1.
Next Rnd: Knit.
Work these two rnds a total of 2 (5, 5, 9, 11, 11, 11) more times. 96 (106, 118, 130, 142, 154, 166) sts.

Divide for legs: K to last 3 sts before BOR, Place next 3 sts on stitch holder/scrap yarn, remove BOR M, place next 3 sts on the same stitch holder/scrap yarn (6 sts total), K42 (47, 53, 59, 65, 71, 77), place next 6 sts on stitch holder/scrap yarn, place remaining 42 (47, 53, 59, 65, 71, 77) sts on stitch holder/scrap yarn to be knit later.

Legs

The left leg is worked using the 42 (47, 53, 59, 65, 71, 77) sts currently on the needles. CO 0 (1, 1, 1, 1, 1, 1) stitch and join to work in the rnd. 42 (48, 54, 60, 66, 72, 78) sts. Work in St st for 0.5 (0.5, 0.5, 0.5, 0.5, 0.5, 0.5)" / 1.5 (1.5, 1.5, 1.5, 1.5, 1.5, 1.5) cm.

Begin working Chart A. Work Rnds 1–30 1 (1, 1, 1, 2, 2, 2) times, then Rnds 1–7 (1–14, 1–14, 1–22, – –, 1–7, 1–14) once more. 26 (30, 36, 38, 42, 44, 48) sts rem. If you desire a longer leg, continue working through Chart B as follows: K1 (0, 0, 1, 0, 1, 0), rep. Chart B until 1 (0, 0, 1, 0, 1, 0) st(s) rem, K1 (0, 0, 1, 0, 1, 0).

Continue working through Chart B until leg measures 1.5 (1.5, 2, 2, 2, 3, 3)" / 4 (4, 5, 5, 5, 7.5, 7.5) cm shorter than desired length.

Cuff

Change to 4.0 mm (US 6) needles.

Decrease Rnd: K1, K0 (2, 0, 0, 2, 2, 0) tog, K to last 3 sts, K1, K0 (2, 0, 0, 2, 2, 0) tog.

Work in K2, P2 ribbing until cuff measures 3 (3, 4, 4, 4, 6, 6)" / 7.5 (7.5, 10, 10, 10, 15, 15) cm. BO loosely.

Right Leg

Place 42 (47, 53, 59, 65, 71, 77) held sts on needle, placing the BO at the inseam. CO 0 (1, 1, 1, 1, 1, 1) and join to work in the rnd. Rep instructions as for left leg.

Finishing

Graft together gusset stitches. Weave in all ends. Blocking is recommended to allow colourwork to relax and lay flat. Make an i-cord for the belt approximately 25 (28, 31, 34, 37, 41, 45)" / 63.5 (71, 79, 86.5, 94, 104, 114.5) cm in length. Weave the belt through the eyelet loops.

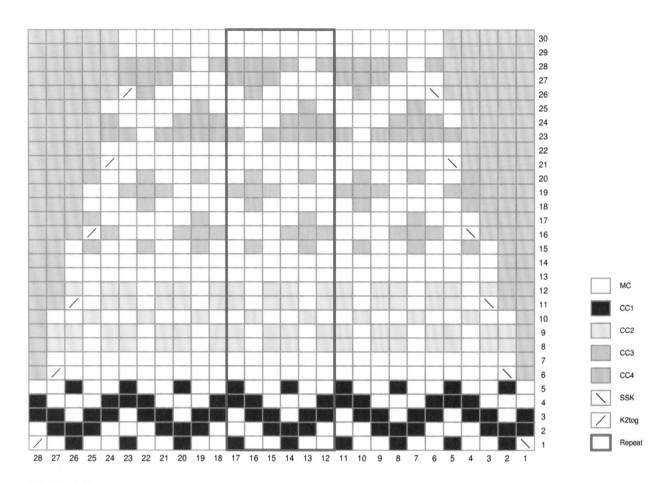

CHART A

Row 1: SSK, K1 CC1, K2 MC, K1 CC1, K2 MC, K1 CC1, K2 MC, K1 CC1, *(K2 MC, K1 CC1) twice; rep. from * to last 12 sts, (K2 MC, K1 CC1) 3 times, K1 MC, K2tog with MC.

Row 2: K3 CC1, K3 MC, K3 CC1, K2 MC, *K1 MC, K3 CC1, K2 MC; rep. from * to last 11 sts, K1 MC, K3 CC1, K3 MC, K3 CC1, K1 MC.

Row 3: (K1 CC1, K1 MC, K1 CC1) 3 times, K1 CC1, K1 MC, *(K2 CC1, K1 MC) twice; rep. from * to last 11 sts, (K2 CC1, K1 MC) 3 times, K2 CC1.

Row 4: K3 MC, K3 CC1, K3 MC, K2 CC1, *K1 CC1, K3 MC, K2 CC1; rep. from * to last 11 sts, K1 CC1, K3 MC, K3 CC1, K3 MC, K1 CC1.

Row 5: (K1 MC, K1 CC1, K1 MC) 3 times, K1 MC, K1 CC1, *(K2 MC, K1 CC1) twice; rep. from * to last 11 sts, (K2 MC, K1 CC1) twice, K5 MC.

Row 6: SSK with MC, K with MC to last 2 sts, K2tog with MC.

Row 7: Knit across with MC.

Row 8: (K2 CC2, K1 MC) 3 times, K1 CC2, *(K1 CC2, K1 MC, K1 CC2) twice; rep. from * to last 10 sts, K1 CC2, K1 MC (K2 CC2, K1 MC) twice, K2 CC2.

Row 9: (K2 CC2, K1 MC) 3 times, K1 CC2, *(K1 CC2, K1 MC, K1 CC2) twice; rep. from * to last 10 sts, K1 CC2, K1 MC (K2 CC2, K1 MC) twice, K2 CC2.

Row 10: (K2 MC, K1 CC2) 3 times, K1 MC, *(K1 MC, K1 CC2, K1 MC) twice; rep. from * to last 10 sts (K1 MC, K1 CC2, K1 MC) twice, K2 MC, K1 CC2, K1 MC.

Row 11: SSK with MC, (K1 MC, K2 CC2) twice, K1 MC, K1 CC2, *(K1 CC2, K1 MC, K1 CC2) twice; rep. from * to last 10 sts, K1 CC2, K1 MC, K2 CC2, K2 MC, K2 CC2, K2tog with MC.

Row 12: (K1 CC2, K1 MC, K1 CC2) 3 times, *(K1 CC2, K1 MC, K1 CC2) twice; rep. from * to last 9 sts, K1 CC2, (K1 MC, K2 CC2, K1 MC) twice.

Row 13: Knit across in MC.

Row 14: Knit across in MC.

Row 15: (K1 MC, K1 CC3, K1 MC) 3 times, *(K1 MC, K1 CC3, K1 MC) twice; rep. from * to last 9 sts, (K1 MC, K1 CC3, K1 MC) 3 times.

Row 16: SSK with MC, K1 MC, K3 CC3, K3 MC, *K3 CC3, K3 MC; rep. from * to last 9 sts, K3 CC3, K3 MC, K1 CC3, K2tog with MC.

Row 17: K3 MC, K1 CC3, K4 MC, *K1 MC, K1 CC3, K4 MC; rep. from * to last 8 sts, K1 MC, K1 CC3, K5 MC, K1 CC3.

Row 18: K1 CC3, K5 MC, K1 CC3, K1 MC, *K4 MC, K1 CC3, K1 MC; rep. from * to last 8 sts, K4 MC, K1 CC3, K3 MC.

Row 19: K2 CC3, K3 MC, K3 CC3, *K3 MC, K3 CC3; rep. from * to last 8 sts, K3 MC, K3 CC3, K2 MC.

Row 20: (K1 CC3, K2 MC) twice, K1 CC3, K1 MC, *(K1 MC, K1 CC3, K1 MC) twice; rep. from * to last 8 sts, (K1 MC, K1 CC3, K1 MC) twice, K1 MC, K1 CC3.

Row 21: SSK, K to last 2 sts, K2tog in MC.

Row 22: Knit across in MC.

Row 23: K5 CC4, K1 MC, K1 CC4, *K4 CC4, K1 MC, K1 CC4; rep. from * to last 7 sts, K4 CC4, K1 MC, K2 CC4.

Row 24: K1 MC, K3 CC4, K3 MC, *K3 CC4, K3 MC; rep. from * to last 7 sts, K3 CC4, K3 MC, K1 CC4.

Row 25: K2 MC, K1 CC4, K4 MC, *K1 MC, K1 CC4, K4 MC; rep. from * to last 7 sts, K1 MC, K1 CC4, K5 MC.

Row 26: SSK with MC, K3 MC, K1 CC4, K1 MC, *K4 MC, K1 CC4, K1 MC; rep. from * to last 7 sts, K4 MC, K1 CC4, K2tog with MC.

Row 27: K3 MC, K3 CC4, *K3 MC, K3 CC4; rep. from * to last 6 sts, K3 MC, K3 CC4.

Row 28: K1 CC4, K1 MC, K4 CC4, *K1 CC4, K1 MC, K4 CC4; rep. from * to last 6 sts, K1 CC4, K1 MC, K4 CC4.

Row 29: Knit across in MC.

Row 30: Knit across in MC.

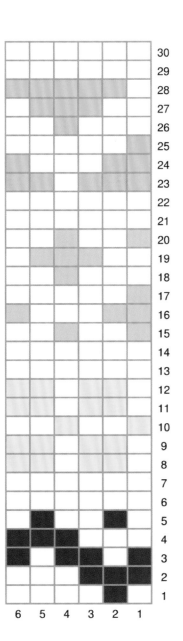

CHART B

Row 1: K1 MC, K1 CC1, K4 MC.

Row 2: K3 CC1, K3 MC.

Row 3: K1 CC1, K1 MC, K2 CC1, K1 MC, K1 CC1.

Row 4: K3 MC, K3 CC1.

Row 5: K1 MC, K1 CC1, K2 MC, K1 CC1, K1 MC.

Rows 6–7: K with MC.

Rows 8–9: K1 MC, K2 CC2, K1 MC, K2 CC2.

Row 10: K1 CC2, K2 MC, K1 CC2, K2 MC.

Rows 11–12: K1 MC, K2 CC2, K1 MC, K2 CC2.

Rows 13–14: K with MC.

Row 15: K1 CC3, K2 MC, K1 CC3, K2 MC.

Row 16: K2 CC3, K3 MC, K1 CC3.

Row 17: K1 CC3, K5 MC.

Row 18: K3 MC, K1 CC3, K2 MC.

Row 19: K2 MC, K3 CC3, K1 MC.

Row 20: K1 CC3, K2 MC, K1 CC3, K2 MC.

Rows 21–22: K with MC.

Row 23: K3 CC4, K1 MC, K2 CC4.

Row 24: K2 CC4, K3 MC, K1 CC4.

Row 25: K1 CC4, K5 MC.

Row 26: K3 MC, K1 CC4, K2 MC.

Row 27: K2 MC, K3 CC4, K1 MC.

Row 28: K1 MC, K5 CC4.

Rows 29–30: K with MC.

BUNDLE
A one-piece bunting suit

Designed for babies and toddlers, this snowsuit is ideal for cooler temperatures, no matter the time of year. The natural stretch of knit fabric allows for movement, and is also safe for car seats and strollers. The suit is knit from the top down and features an all-over texture, raglan increases to create the sleeves, and a hood with a short row band for extra warmth.

SKILL LEVEL
Intermediate

Skills required:
knitting flat, knitting in the round, increasing, decreasing, seaming, picking up and knitting stitches, buttonholes, short rows

MATERIALS
Approx 567 (630, 693, 762) yds / 518 (576, 634, 697) m of worsted-weight yarn. Sample shown in Cascade 220 Superwash, col. 1910 "Summer Sky Heather," 220 yds / 201 m per 100 g ball.

4.0 mm (US 6) needles for knitting flat
4.0 mm (US 6) DPNs or a 32" / 80 cm circular needle for magic loop
4.5 mm (US 7) needles for knitting flat
4.5 mm (US 7) DPNs or a 32" / 80 cm circular needle for magic loop
Or size required to obtain gauge

Tapestry needle
4 (5, 5, 6) buttons; sample shows 0.75" / 2 cm toggle buttons

GAUGE
20 sts and 27 rows = 4" / 10 cm
In stitch pattern, with 4.5 mm (US 7) needles

SIZES
0–6 mo (6–12 mo, 1–2 yrs, 2–3 yrs)
Finished chest measurement: 17 (18.5, 20, 22.5)" / 43 (47, 51, 57) cm

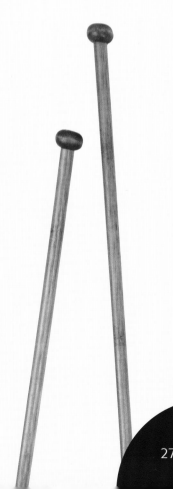

INSTRUCTIONS

Hood

With 4.5 mm (US 7) needles for working flat, CO 44 (48, 56, 64) sts using the long-tail CO (see Special Techniques). Purl 1 row.

Begin working in pattern:

Row 1 (RS): *K3, P1; rep from * to end.

Row 2 (WS): Purl.

Row 3: Knit.

Row 4: Purl.

Row 5: *K1, P1, K2; rep from * to end.

Rows 6–8: as Rows 2–4.

Work in patt until hood measures 8 (8.5, 9, 9)" / 20.5, 21.5, 23, 23) cm from CO edge, ending after Row 2 or Row 6 of the patt.

Dec Row: K18 (20, 24, 24), K2tog 4 (4, 4, 8) times, K18 (20, 24, 24). 40 (44, 52, 56) sts rem.

Continue working in patt until piece measures 9 (9.5, 10.5, 11)" / 23 (24, 26.5, 28) cm from CO edge, ending after Row 4 or Row 8.

Raglan Increases

Row 1 (RS): Work in patt for 4 (5, 6, 7) sts, PM, work in patt for 7 (7, 9, 9) sts, PM, work in patt for 18 (20, 22, 24) sts, PM, work 7 (7, 9, 9) sts in patt, PM, work 4 (5, 6, 7) sts in patt.

Row 2 (WS): Purl.

Row 3: *Work in patt to 1 st before M, M1L, K1, sl M, K1, M1R; rep. from * 3 more times, work in patt to end.

Row 4: Purl.

Continue working Rows 3–4 until you have 18 (20, 22, 25) sts per front, 35 (37, 41, 45) sts per sleeve and 46 (50, 54, 60) sts for the back. 152 (164, 180, 200) sts total.

Divide for Body

Work in patt to first M, remove M, place next 35 (37, 41, 45) sts on stitch holder/scrap yarn, CO 1, remove M, work in patt across back sts to next M, remove M, place next 35 (37, 41, 45) sts on stitch holder/scrap yarn, CO 1, remove M, work in patt to end of row. 84 (92, 100, 112) sts rem.

Continue working in patt until body measures 6.5 (7, 7.75, 8.5)" / 16.5 (18, 19.5, 21.5) cm from underarm, ending after a WS row.

Next Row: Work in patt to end of row, CO 8 (8, 8, 8) sts using the backward loop method (see Special Techniques). Place BOR M and join to work in the rnd. 92 (100, 108, 120) sts.

Continue working in patt, in the rnd, until body measures 8.25 (9, 10.25, 12)" / 21 (23, 26, 30.5) cm from underarm, or until body reaches desired length.

Dividing for Legs

Work across in patt to the last 4 sts. Work the next 46 (50, 54, 60) sts in patt (removing BOR M), place next 46 (50, 54, 60) sts on stitch holder/scrap yarn. CO 1, place BOR M, CO 1, join to work in the rnd. 48 (52, 56, 62) sts on needle.

Work in patt for 1.75 (2, 2.5, 3.5)" / 4.5 (5, 6.5, 9) cm.

Dec Rnd: K1, SSK, work in patt to last 3 sts, K2tog, K1. 46 (50, 54, 60) sts.

Work 5 rnds in established patt.

Rep these 6 rnds four more times. 38 (42, 46, 52) sts rem.

Work in patt until leg measures 7.5 (8.5, 9.5, 10.5)" / 19 (21.5, 24, 26.5) cm from divide, or until the leg is 2 (2, 3, 3)" / 5 (5, 7.5, 7.5) cm shorter than desired length.

Switch to 4.0 mm (US 6) needles for working in the round. Work in K1, P1 ribbing for 2 (2, 3, 3)" / 5 (5, 7.5, 7.5) cm. BO loosely. Cut yarn, leaving a 6" / 15 cm tail.

Right Leg

Place held sts onto working needle. CO 1, place BOR, CO 1, join to work in the rnd. 48 (52, 56, 62) sts on needle.

Repeat leg instructions.

Sleeves

Place 35 (37, 41, 45) sts on working needle. Work across sts in patt, PU 2 sts in the underarm, place BOR M, PU 1 stitch in the underarm, work in patt to the end of the rnd. 38 (40, 44, 48) sts on needle.

0–6-month size only: K1, SSK, K to last 3 sts, K2tog, K1. 36 (40, 44, 48) sts.

Work in patt for 0.75 (1, 1.25, 1.75)" / 2(2.5, 3, 4.5) cm.

Dec Rnd: K1, SSK, work in patt to the last 3 sts, K2tog, K1. 36 (38, 42, 46) sts.
Work 3 rnds in patt.

Rep these 4 rnds four more times. 26 (30, 34, 38) sts rem.

Work in patt until sleeve measures 5 (6, 7, 8)" / 12.5 (15, 18, 20.5) cm from underarm or until it reaches 1.5" / 4 cm shorter than desired length.

Change to 4.0 mm (US 6) needles for working in the round. Work in K1, P1 ribbing for 1.5" / 4 cm. BO loosely. Cut yarn, leaving a 6" / 15 cm tail.

Repeat instructions for second sleeve.

Button Band

Before starting the button band, seam the top of the hood together using the horizontal seaming method (see Special Techniques).

Using 4.0 mm (US 6) needles for knitting flat, start at the bottom right side and PU and knit sts at a rate of 2 sts per 3 rows. You should have approximately 174 (188, 204, 224) sts on the needles. *These will differ if you increased or decreased lengths from the pattern.*

Next Row (WS): K87 (94, 102, 112), place centre M, K87 (94, 102, 112). *If your stitch counts are different from these, this marker should be at the very top of the hood, where the two sides were joined.*

Short Rows:

Row 1 (RS): K to centre M, Sl M, K 40 (42, 47, 49), turn work.

Row 2 (WS): K to centre M, Sl M, K40 (42, 47, 49), turn work.

Row 3 (RS): K to 5 sts before gap, turn work.

Row 4 (WS): K to 5 sts before gap, turn work.

Repeat Rows 3–4 five more times. There should be 20 (24, 34, 38) unworked stitches in the centre, 10 (12, 17, 19) at either side of the centre marker.

Next, starting where you left off from the last short row, knit to the end of the row—you do not need to pick up any stitches to fill gaps from short rows—the garter stitch will hide this!

Knit 3 more rows in garter stitch.

Buttonhole Row (RS): K127 (135, 150, 160), *K2tog, YO, K 9 (8, 9, 8); rep from * 2 (3, 3, 4) more times, K2tog, YO, K to end of row. *If your original button band stitch counts differ, start the buttonholes from the point where the hood meets the body. Divide as evenly as possible over 4 (5, 5, 6) to place the buttonholes.*

Knit 6 more rows in garter. BO loosely kwise on the WS. Cut yarn, leaving a 6" / 15 cm tail.

Finishing

Overlap the button bands and seam them together with the CO sts from where you joined the body to knit in the round. Weave in all ends. Blocking is recommended to let the stitch pattern relax. Sew on buttons.

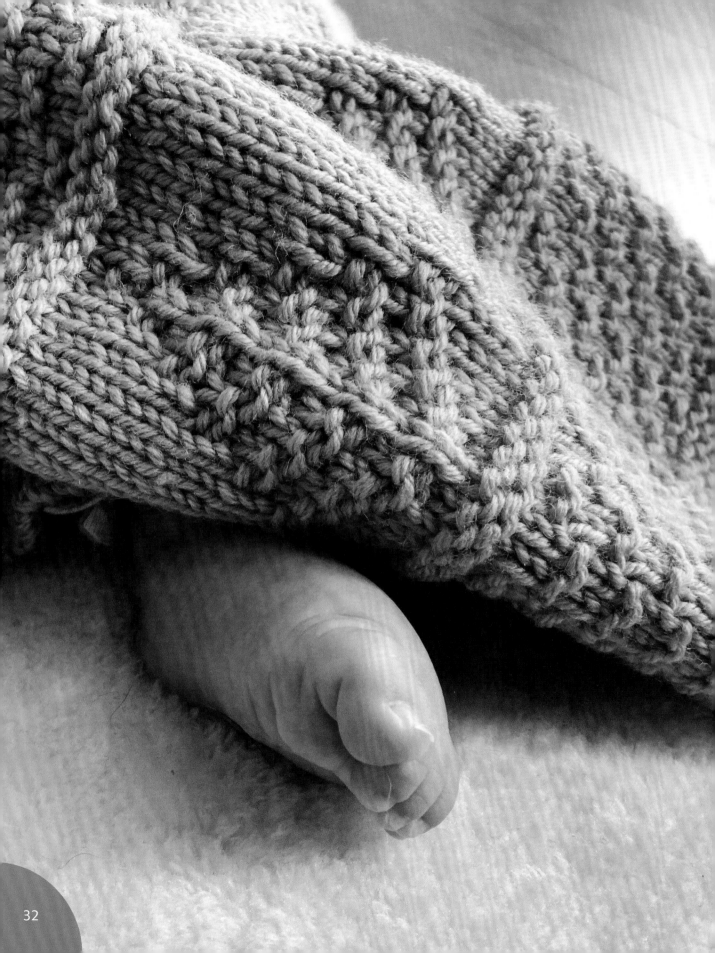

ISLANDER A Guernsey-inspired blanket

From one island to another! This blanket is inspired by the iconic Guernsey or Gansey sweater, featuring bands of knit-purl textures: staggered bricks, trees, and classic ribbing, separated by purled bands and accented with a garter stitch border. This pattern includes charted and written instructions and three different sizes, making it an easily customized knit.

SKILL LEVEL
Beginner

Skills required:
working flat, knit and purl textures, chart reading, long-tail cast on

MATERIALS
Approximately 660 (925, 1375) yds / 604 (846, 1257) m worsted-weight yarn. Sample shown in Cascade 220 Superwash, col. 250 "Laurel Green," 220 yds / 201 m per 100 g ball.

4.0 mm (US 6) needles for knitting flat

Two (2) stitch markers
Tapestry needle

GAUGE
21 sts and 32 rows = 4" / 10 cm
In brick pattern, after blocking

SIZES
Sizes: Lap (Crib, Throw)
Width: 22 (29.5, 43)" / 53 (75, 109) cm
Length: 27 (39, 50.5)" / 69 (98, 128) cm

Purled Band: Knit 2 rows, purl 2 rows.

Tree Band: K5 (6, 7), Sl M, insert Chart B, Sl M, K5 (6, 7).
Work Rows 1–20 of Chart B.

Purled Band: Knit 2 rows, purl 2 rows.

Brick Band: RS Row: K5 (6, 7), Sl M, K0 (1, 0), insert Chart A, K0 (1, 0), Sl M, K5 (6, 7).
WS Row: K5 (6, 7), Sl M, P0 (1, 0), insert Chart A, P0 (1, 0), Sl M, K5 (6, 7).
Work Rows 1–4 of Chart A five times.

Purled Band: Knit 2 rows, purl 2 rows.

Ribbed Band: RS Row: K5 (6, 7), Sl M, K0 (1, 0), insert Chart C, K0 (1, 0), Sl M, K5 (6, 7).
WS Row: K5 (6, 7), Sl M, P0 (1, 0), insert Chart C, P0 (1, 0), Sl M, K5 (6, 7).
Work Rows 1–2 of Chart C 11 times.

Purled Band: Knit 2 rows, purl 2 rows.

Rep from the first brick band 1 (2, 3) more time(s).

Work the brick band one more time as follows:
RS Row: K5 (6, 7), Sl M, K0 (1, 0), insert Chart A, K0 (1, 0), Sl M, K5 (6, 7).
WS Row: K5 (6, 7), Sl M, P0 (1, 0), insert Chart A, P0 (1, 0), Sl M, K5 (6, 7).
Work Rows 1–4 of Chart A five times.

Top Border

Work 9 (11, 13) rows of garter stitch for the top border. BO loosely kwise on the WS.

INSTRUCTIONS

Bottom Border

CO 110 (154, 226) sts using the long-tail CO method (see Special Techniques). Work 8 (10, 12) rows in garter stitch.

Band Set-up Row (WS): K5 (6, 7), PM, K until 5 (6, 7) sts rem, PM, K5 (6, 7).

Pattern Bands

The pattern is created using three alternating charts separated by purled bands. Following the row instructions for each chart, work the patterned bands in the following order:

Brick Band: RS Row: K5 (6, 7), Sl M, K0 (1, 0), insert Chart A, K0 (1, 0), Sl M, K5 (6, 7).
WS Row: K5 (6, 7), Sl M, P0 (1, 0), insert Chart A, P0 (1, 0), Sl M, K5 (6, 7).
Work Rows 1–4 of Chart A five times.

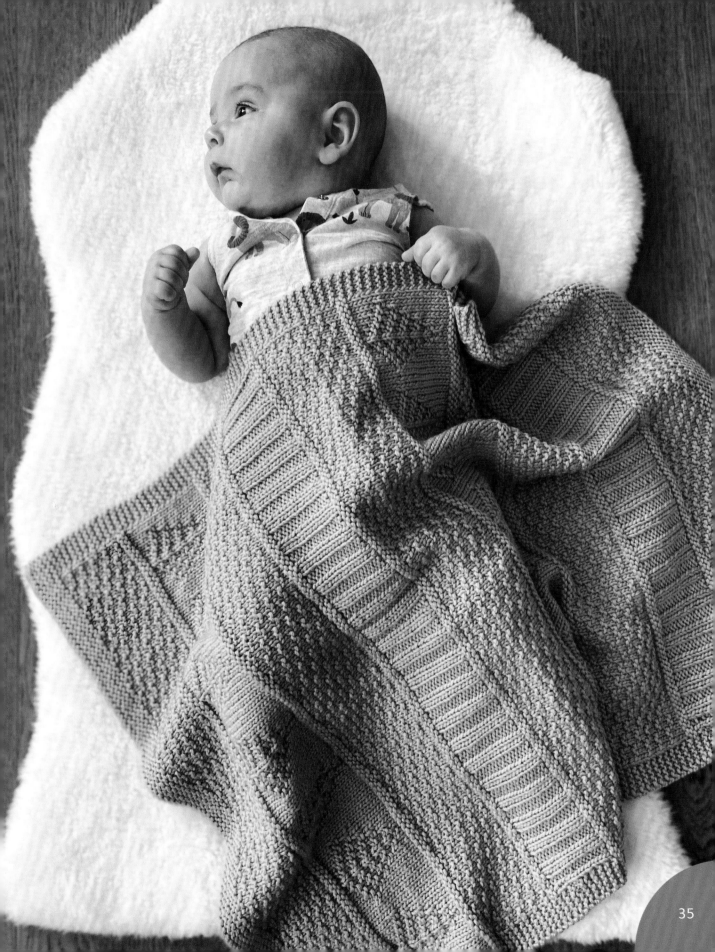

Finishing

Weave in all ends. For best results, block using blocking wires to maintain straight edges.

CHART A

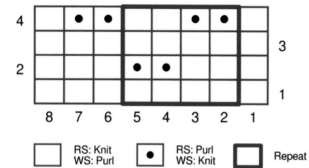

Row 1 (RS): Knit.

Row 2 (WS): P3, *K2, P2; rep from * to 1 (2, 1) st(s) before M, P1, continue to row instructions.

Row 3: Knit.

Row 4: P1, K2, *P2, K2; rep from * to 1 (2, 1) st(s) before M, P1, continue to row instructions.

CHART B

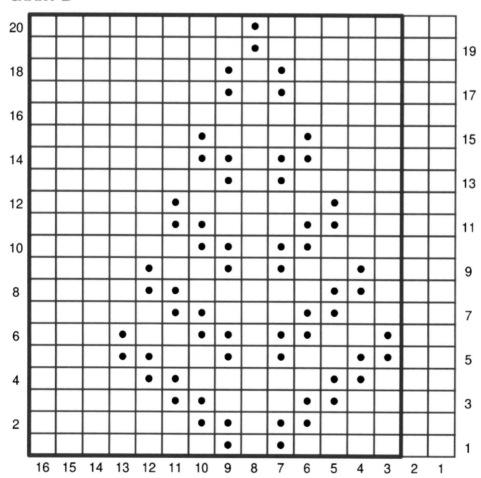

Row 1 (RS): K2, *K4, P1, K1, P1, K7; rep from * to M.

Row 2 (WS): *P6, K2, P1, K2, P3; rep from * to 2 sts before M, P2.

Row 3: K2, *K2, P2, K3, P2, K5; rep from * to M.

Row 4: *P4, K2, P5, K2, P1; rep from * to 2 sts before M, P2.

Row 5: K2, *P2, K2, P1, K1, P1, K2, P2, K3; rep from * to M.

Row 6: *P3, K1, P2, K2, P1, K2, P2, K1; rep from * to 2 sts before M, P2.

Row 7: K2, *K2, P2, K3, P2, K5 rep from * to M.

Row 8: *P4, K2, P5, K2, P1; rep from * to 2 sts before M, P2.

Row 9: K2, *K1, P1, K2, P1, K1, P1, K2, P1, K4; rep from * to M.

Row 10: *P6, K2, P1, K2, P3; rep from * to 2 sts before M, P2.

Row 11: K2, *K2, P2, K3, P2, K5; rep from * to M.

Row 12: *P5, K1, P5, K1, P2; rep from * to 2 sts before M, P2.

Row 13: K2, *K4, P1, K1, P1, K7; rep from * to M.

Row 14: *P6, K2, P1, K2, P3; rep from * to 2 sts before M, P2.

Row 15: K2, *K3, P1, K3, P1, K6; rep from * to M.

Row 16: Purl.

Row 17: K2, *K4, P1, K1, P1, K7; rep from * to M.

Row 18: *P7, K1, P1, K1, P4; rep from * to 2 sts before M, P2.

Row 19: K2, *K5, P1, K8; rep from * to M.

Row 20: *P8, K1, P5; rep from * to 2 sts before M, P2.

CHART C

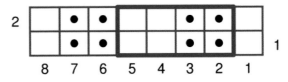

Row 1 (RS): K1, *P2, K2; rep. from * to 3 (4, 3) sts before M, P2, K1, continue to row instructions.

Row 2 (WS): P1, K2, *P2, K2; rep. from * to 1 (2, 1) st(s) before M, P1, continue to row instructions.

BOREAL A hooded jacket

This jacket is designed for the crisp morning air, changing colours, and autumn leaves crunching underfoot. The warm but lightweight fabric makes for the perfect outer layer for cooler temperatures and outdoor activities. The oversized jacket, knit from the top down, features raglan increases, textured cuffs and bands, and a hood to keep little heads toasty warm.

SKILL LEVEL
Experienced beginner

Skills required:
knitting in the round, picking up stitches, seaming, increasing and decreasing, knit and purl textures, buttonholes

MATERIALS
Approximately 365 (405, 450, 495, 545, 600, 660) yds / 334 (370, 411, 453, 498, 549, 604) m bulky-weight yarn. Sample shown in Cascade Eco col. 7098, 478 yds / 437 m per 250 g skein.

6.0 mm (US 10) needles for knitting flat
6.0 mm (US 10) DPNs or a 32" / 80 cm circular needle for magic loop for knitting in the round
Or size required to obtain gauge

Tapestry needle
2 (2, 3, 3, 3, 4, 4) toggle buttons

GAUGE
16.5 sts and 25 rows = 4" / 10 cm
In stockinette stitch

SIZES
0–6 months (6–12 months, 1–2, 2–4, 4–6, 6–8, 8–10)
Finished chest measurements: 18 (21, 22, 24, 26, 27, 28)" / 46 (53, 56, 61, 66, 69, 71) cm
This garment is meant to be worn with 0–3" / 0–7.5 cm of positive ease

INSTRUCTIONS

Hood

With 6.0 mm (US 10) needles for working flat, CO 36 (44, 48, 50, 54, 54, 56) sts. Work in St st for 8 (9, 9, 10, 10, 11, 11)" / 20 (23, 23, 25, 25, 28, 28) cm.

Dec Row: K14 (16, 18, 19, 21, 21, 22), K2tog 4 (6, 6, 6, 6, 6, 6) times, K14 (16, 18, 19, 21, 21, 22). 32 (38, 42, 44, 48, 48, 50) sts rem.

Continue working in St st until the hood measures 8.5 (9.5, 10.5, 11, 11, 12.5, 13)" / 22 (24, 27, 28, 28, 32, 33) cm from CO edge, ending after a WS row.

Sleeve Increases

Set Up (RS): K4 (4, 4, 5, 5, 5, 5), PM, K5 (6, 7, 7, 7, 7, 7), PM, K14 (18, 20, 20, 24, 24, 26), PM, K5 (6, 7, 7, 7, 7, 7), PM, K4 (4, 4, 5, 5, 5, 5).
Next Row (WS): Purl.

Next, start working the increases as follows:
Row 1: *K to 1 stitch before M, M1L, K1, Sl M, M1R; rep. from * three more times. 8 sts increased.
Row 2: Purl.

Repeat Rows 1–2 until you have 128 (150, 162, 172, 184, 192, 202) sts on your needles: 16 (18, 19, 21, 22, 23, 24) for each front, 29 (34, 37, 39, 41, 43, 45) for each sleeve, and 38 (46, 50, 52, 58, 60, 64) for the back.

Dividing the sleeves: K to M, remove M, slip the next 29 (34, 37, 39, 41, 43, 45) to scrap yarn/ stitch holder, CO 2 sts using the backward loop method (see Special Techniques), K to next M, remove M, slip the next 29 (34, 37, 39, 41, 43, 45) to scrap yarn/ stitch holder, CO 2 sts, K to end. Total stitches on needles: 74 (86, 92, 98, 106, 110, 116).
Next row: Purl.

Body

Work in St st until body measures 7 (8, 9, 10, 11, 13, 14)" / 18 (20, 23, 25, 28, 33, 36) cm from underarm, or until it measures 1.5 (1.5, 2, 2, 3, 3, 4)" / 4 (4, 5, 5, 8, 8, 10) cm shorter than desired length, ending after a WS row.

Next, work the texture pattern as follows:
Row 1 (RS): *K1, P1; rep. from * to the end of the row.
Row 2 (WS): Purl.
Row 3: *P1, K1; rep. from * to the end of the row.
Row 4: Purl.

Continue working Rows 1–4 until the patterned section measures 1.5 (1.5, 2, 2, 3, 3, 4)" / 4 (4, 5, 5, 8, 8, 10) cm, total length from underarm 8.5 (9.5, 11, 12, 14, 16, 18)" / 22 (24, 28, 30, 36, 41, 46) cm, or until you reach the desired length.

Rolled Edge

To finish the body, work the following rows:

Row 1 (RS): Purl.

Row 2 (WS): Knit.

Row 3: Purl.

BO loosely kwise. Cut yarn, leaving a 6" / 15 cm tail.

Sleeves

Starting with the underarm stitches, place 29 (34, 37, 39, 41, 43, 45) sleeve stitches onto working needles.

Set up: K across sleeve stitches, PU 2 sts from the underarm CO sts, place BOR M, join to work in the round. 31 (36, 39, 41, 43, 45, 47) sts.

Dec Rnd: K to last 2 (0, 2, 2, 2, 2, 2) sts, K 2 (0, 2, 2, 2, 2, 2) tog. 30 (36, 38, 40, 42, 44, 46) sts rem.

Work in St st until sleeve measures 5 (6, 6.5, 7.5, 8.5, 9.5, 9.5)" / 13 (15, 17, 19, 22, 24, 24) or until the sleeve measures 1.5 (1.5, 2, 2, 3, 3, 4)" / 4 (4, 5, 5, 8, 8, 10) cm shorter than desired length.

Next, work the texture pattern as follows:

Rnd 1: *K1, P1; rep from * to the end of the rnd.

Rnd 2: Knit.

Rnd 3: *P1, K1; rep from * to the end of the row.

Rnd 4: Knit.

Continue working Rnds 1–4 until the patterned section measures 1.5 (1.5, 2, 2, 3, 3, 4)" / 4 (4, 5, 5, 8, 8, 10) cm, total length from underarm 6.5 (7.5, 8.5, 9.5, 11.5, 12.5, 13.5)" / 17 (19, 22, 24, 29, 32, 34) cm, or until you reach the desired length.

To finish the sleeve, purl 3 rnds. BO loosely pwise. Repeat for the second sleeve.

Front Band

Before picking up stitches for the band, seam the hood. Fold the hood together and seam using your preferred method. For best results, try the horizontal seaming method (see Special Techniques).

Starting at the bottom right edge of the sweater, begin picking up stitches at a rate of 3 sts for every 4 rows, ensuring an even number of stitches. Approximately 200 (226, 252, 270, 300, 326, 354) sts.

Knit 1 row on the WS.

Begin working texture pattern as follows:

Row 1 (RS): *K1, P1; rep from * to the end of the row.

Row 2 (WS): Purl.

Row 3: *P1, K1; rep from * to the end of the row.

Row 4: Purl.

Continue working Rows 1–4 until the band measures 2 (2, 2.5, 2.5, 3.5, 3.5, 4.5)" / 5 (5, 6, 6, 9, 9, 11) cm wide, ending after a RS row.

Next Row (WS): Purl along the WS of the left band and around the hood, stopping at the point where the hood meets the shoulders of the jacket, approximately 139 (156, 172, 180, 197, 205, 213) sts for proper row gauge, PM, purl to end.

Buttonhole Row (RS): Work in patt until 14 (14, 30, 30, 30, 44, 44) sts before M, YO, K2tog, *K 10 (10, 12, 12, 12, 12, 12), YO, K2tog; rep. from * to M, sl M, work in patt to end.

Next Row (WS): Purl across.

To finish the bands, work a rolled edge as follows:
Row 1 (RS): Purl.
Row 2 (WS): Knit.
Row 3: Purl.

BO loosely kwise.

Finishing

Weave in all ends. Blocking is recommended to allow the texture pattern to relax. Attach buttons to left band along the pick-up row (not the edge).

LUPINE A sweet little dress

While ideal for warm summer months, this little dress can be easily layered to be worn any time of year. The dress features eyelet-lace patterning in the skirt and a garter stitch bodice. This piece is worked from the bottom up and uses box pleats to bring the fabric in for the top. Finally, the dress can be sleeveless or include capped sleeves—knitter's choice!

SKILL LEVEL
Intermediate

Skills required:
working in the round, lace, increasing and decreasing, picking up stitches, short rows, crochet grafting

MATERIALS
Approximately 424 (470, 522, 574, 633, 696, 765) yds / 388 (430, 477, 525, 579, 636, 700) m fingering-weight yarn. Sample shown in Julie Asselin Fino in col. "Week End," 400 yds / 366 m per 115 g skein.

3.5 mm (US 4) needles for knitting in the round
3.5 mm (US 4) needles for knitting flat
2 3.5 mm DPNs for box pleat
Or size required to obtain gauge

Tapestry needle   Stitch marker
Stitch holder   2.75 mm (US 2) crochet hook for finishing

GAUGE
24.5 sts and 41 rnds = 4" / 10 cm
In garter stitch, worked in the round with 3.5 mm (US 4) needles, after blocking

26.5 sts and 38 rnds = 4" / 10 cm
In stockinette stitch, worked in the round with 3.5 mm (US 4) needles, after blocking

SIZES
Sizes: 0–6 mo (6–12 mo, 1–2, 2–4, 4–6, 6–8, 8–10)
Finished chest measurement: 16 (18, 20, 22, 24, 26, 28)" / 41 (46, 51, 56, 61, 66, 71) cm
Meant to be fitted on the chest with 0–2.5" / 0–6.5 cm of negative ease

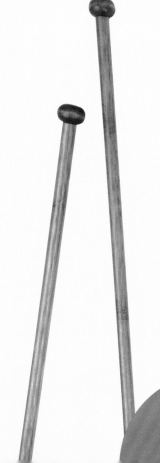

INSTRUCTIONS

Hem

Using 3.5 mm (US 4) needles, CO 192 (208, 240, 256, 288, 320, 352) sts. Place BOR M and join to work in the rnd.

Rnd 1: Purl across.
Rnd 2: Knit across.
Repeat Rnds 1–2 eight more times.

Lace Edge

The lace design at the bottom of the dress is worked using Chart A. Work Rnds 1–18 of Chart A, repeating the lace pattern 12 (13, 15, 16, 18, 20, 22) times across the rnd.

Skirt

Rnds 1–12: Knit.
Rnd 13: *K14, K2tog, YO; rep across the rnd.
Rnds 14–26: Knit.
Rnd 27: *K7, YO, K2tog, K7; rep across the rnd.

Work Rnds 1–27 a total of 2 (2, 2, 2, 3, 4, 5, 5) times. Next, work Rnds 1–13 a total of 0 (1, 1, 1, 0, 0, 1) time. Finally, work 8 (6, 12, 12, 12, 12, 12) rnds in St st.

Box Pleats

The next round will use box pleats to decrease the stitch count for the bodice. To work the box pleats, use your working needles and the extra DPNs of the same size.

Pleat Rnd: K6 (6, 7, 8, 9, 10, 11), work Pleat A (see below), work Pleat B (see below), K12 (12, 14, 16, 18, 20, 22), work Pleat A, work Pleat B, K12 (12, 14, 16, 18, 20, 22), work Pleat A, work Pleat B, K12 (12, 14, 16, 18, 20, 22), work Pleat A, work Pleat B, K6 (6, 7, 8, 9, 10, 11). 96 (104, 120, 128, 144, 160, 176) sts rem.

Pleat A

Slip 6 (7, 8, 8, 9, 10, 11) sts onto DPN #1, slip 6 (7, 8, 8, 9, 10, 11) sts onto DPN #2. Fold work in a Z shape so that DPN #1 and DPN #2 are held in the FRONT, parallel to each other with the wrong sides together. With your working needle, K2tog by knitting the first stitches from DPN #1 and DPN #2 together 0 (1, 1, 0, 0, 0, 0) time(s). Next, K3tog by knitting the first stitches from DPN #1, DPN #2, and the LH needle together 6 (6, 7, 8, 9, 10, 11) times. This forms the first half of the first box pleat.

Pleat B

Slip 6 (7, 8, 8, 9, 10, 11) sts onto DPN #1, slip 6 (7, 8, 8, 9, 10, 11) sts onto DPN #2. Fold work in a Z shape so that DPN #1 and DPN #2 are held in the BACK, parallel to each other with the right sides together. With your working needle, K3tog by knitting the first stitches from DPN #1, DPN #2, and the LH needle together 6 (6, 7, 8, 9, 10, 11) times. Next, K2tog by knitting the first stitches from DPN #1 and DPN #2 together 0 (1, 1, 0, 0, 0, 0) time(s). This forms the second half of the first box pleat.

Bodice

Work in garter stitch until the bodice measures 1 (1, 1.25, 1.5, 1.5, 1.75, 2)" / 2.5 (2.5, 3, 4, 4, 4.5, 5) cm from the first purl rnd, ending after a purl rnd.

Divide the sts for the front and back: K48 (52, 60, 64, 72, 80, 88) sts for the front, place the next 48 (52, 60, 64, 72, 80, 88) sts on spare needles / scrap yarn to be worked later.

Continue the front by working flat in garter stitch until the front measures 1.5 (1.5, 2, 2, 2.5, 2.5, 3)" / 4 (4, 5, 5, 6.5, 6.5, 7.5) cm from the divide, 2.5 (2.5, 3.25, 3.5, 4, 4.25, 5)" / 6.5, 6.5, 8, 9, 10, 11, 13) cm in total from the beginning of the bodice, ending after a WS row.

Neck Shaping

Next Row: K12 (12, 14, 15, 17, 19, 21), BO 24 (28, 32, 34, 38, 42, 46), K12 (12, 14, 15, 17, 19, 21). Place sts for left strap on stitch holder / scrap yarn. Continue working the right strap as follows:

Row 1 (WS): K to end.
Row 2 (RS): SSK, K to end (1 stitch dec).

Continue working Rows 1–2 until 8 (9, 9, 10, 11, 12, 13) sts rem.

Next, continue working in garter stitch until the strap measures 1.5 (1.5, 2, 2, 2.5, 2.5, 3)" / 4 (4, 5, 5, 6.5, 6.5, 7.5) cm from the beginning of the neckline shaping, 4 (4, 5.25, 5.5, 6.5, 6.75, 8)" / 10 (10, 13.5, 14, 16.5, 17, 20.5) cm from the beginning of the bodice, ending after a WS row.

Place live stitches on holder while you work the left strap. Place the held stitches for the left strap onto working needles. With the WS facing, join yarn and begin working the strap as follows:

Row 1 (WS): K to end.
Row 2 (RS): K to last 2 sts, K2tog (1 stitch dec).
Continue working Rows 1–2 until 8 (9, 9, 10, 11, 12, 13) sts rem.

Next, continue working in garter stitch until the strap measures 1.5 (1.5, 2, 2, 2.5, 2.5, 3)" / 4 (4, 5, 5, 6.5, 6.5, 7.5) cm from the beginning of the neckline shaping, 4 (4, 5.25, 5.5, 6.5, 6.75, 8)" / 10 (10, 13.5, 14, 16.5, 17, 20.5) cm from the beginning of the bodice, ending after a WS row.

Place live stitches on holder while you work the back.

Back

Place held 48 (52, 60, 64, 72, 80, 88) sts on working needles. Work flat in garter stitch until the back measures 4 (4, 5.25, 5.5, 6.5, 6.75, 8)" / 10 (10, 13.5, 14, 16.5, 17, 20.5) cm from the beginning of the bodice.

Next Row: K8 (9, 9, 10, 11, 12, 13), BO 32 (34, 42, 44, 50, 56, 62), K8 (9, 9, 10, 11, 12, 13). Cut yarn, leaving a 15" / 38 cm tail.

Working one side at a time, place the held strap sts onto a working needle and use the kitchener stitch (see Special Techniques) to graft the front and back live stitches together. Once the front and back have been grafted, continue to work the sleeves. If you choose to omit the sleeves, continue to the finishing instructions.

Sleeves

Using needles for working in the rnd, start at the middle of the underarm sts and PU and K33 (33, 44, 44, 55, 55, 66) sts along the edge of the back at a rate of approximately 1 stitch for every 2 rows. Place BOR M and join to work in the rnd.

Rnd 1: Purl around.
Rnd 2: Knit around.
Rnd 3: Purl around.
Rnd 4: K to 3 sts before BOR, turn.
Rnd 5: K to 3 sts before BOR, turn.
Rnd 6: K to 3 sts before gap, turn.
Rnd 7: K to 3 sts before gap, turn.
Rep Rnds 6–7 1 (1, 2, 2, 3, 3, 4) more times.

Rnd 8: K to BOR. *You will not need to do anything to pick up the gaps as the garter stitch fills the gap.*
Rnd 9: Purl around.
Rnd 10: Knit around.
Rep Rnds 9–10 0 (0, 0, 1, 1, 2, 2) more times.

BO pwise loosely, ensuring there is room for stretch. Repeat sleeve instructions for the second sleeve.

Finishing

Starting at the shoulder with the RS facing, use a 2.75 mm (US2) crochet hook and work a single-crochet stitch edge (see Special Techniques) around the edge of the neckline.

If you've omitted the sleeves, work a single crochet edge as above around each armhole, starting at the underarm.

Weave in all ends. For best results, block to open the lace stitch patterns and relax the stitches.

CHART A

Rnd 1: K4, YO, SSK, K3, K2tog, YO, K3, K2tog, YO.

Rnd 2 and all even numbered rnds: Knit.

Rnd 3: YO, SSK, K3, YO, SSK, K1, K2tog, YO, K3, K2tog, YO, K1.

Rnd 5: K1, YO, SSK, K3, YO, CDD, YO, K3, K2tog, YO, K2.

Rnd 7: K2, YO, SSK, K3, YO, SSK, K2, K2tog, YO, K3.

Rnd 9: K3, YO, SSK, K5, K2tog, YO, K4.

Rnd 11: K4, YO, SSK, K3, K2tog, YO, K5.

Rnd 13: K5, YO, SSK, K1, K2tog, YO, K6.

Rnd 15: K6, YO, CDD, YO, K7.

Rnd 17: K7, YO, SSK, K7.

Rnd 18: Knit.

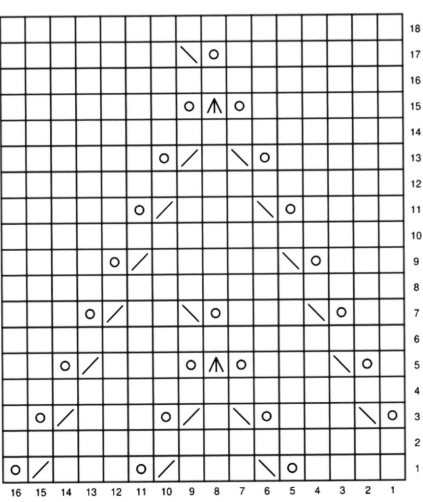

Iceberg *A yoke sweater*

A blend of traditional Shetland and Newfoundland knitting, this sweater is designed to look good for any colour palette, with simple two-colour stranded work for the yoke. The wide neck allows for comfort, while also making dressing and undressing easier. Like any wool sweater, not only does this one look good but it is also a functional outer garment, especially for chilly fall days.

SKILL LEVEL
Intermediate

Skills required: working in the round, stranded colourwork, increasing and decreasing, short rows

MATERIALS
Approximately 350 (389, 432, 480, 528, 581, 639) yds / 320 (356, 395, 349, 483, 531, 584) m worsted-weight yarn. Sample shown in Knit Picks Swish worsted, 110 yds / 100 m per 50 g ball, 321 (356, 396, 440, 484, 532, 585) yds / 294 (326, 362, 402, 443, 486, 535) m in "Dove Heather" (MC) and 15 (16, 18, 20, 22, 24, 27) yds / 14 (15, 16, 18, 20, 22, 25) m each in "White" (CC2) and "Garnet Heather" (CC1).

4.0 mm (US 6) needles for knitting in the round
4.5 mm (US 7) needles for knitting in the round
Or size required to obtain gauge

Tapestry needle
Stitch marker

GAUGE
21 sts and 31 rnds = 4" / 10 cm
In stockinette stitch, worked in the round with 4.5 mm (US 7) needles, after blocking

SIZES
Sizes: 0–6 mo (6–12 mo, 1–2, 2–4, 4–6, 6–8, 8–10)
Finished chest measurement: 18.5 (19.5, 21, 24, 26.5, 29, 30.5)" / 47 (50, 53, 61, 67, 74, 77) cm
Garment is meant to be fitted on the chest with 2–4" / 5–10 cm of positive ease

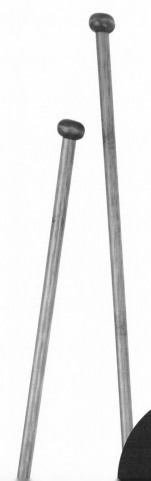

INSTRUCTIONS

Sleeves

Using smaller needles and MC, CO 24 (28, 28, 30, 32, 36, 36) sts. Join to work in the round, being careful not to twist the stitches. Place marker for BOR. Work in K1, P1 ribbing for 1.5 (1.5, 1.5, 2, 2, 2.5, 2.5)" / 3 (3, 3, 5, 5, 6, 6) cm.

Switch to larger needles. Knit 2 rnds.

Increase Rnd: K1, M1L, K to last stitch before BOR, M1R, K1. K 5 rnds.

Repeat these 6 rnds 3 (4, 4, 4, 4, 4, 5) more times. 32 (38, 38, 40, 42, 46, 48) sts total.

Continue working in St st until the sleeve measures 6.5 (7.5, 8.5, 10.5, 11.5, 12.5, 13.5)" / 17 (19, 22, 27, 29, 32, 34) cm from the CO edge, or until you reach the desired length.

BO Round: K to 3 (3, 3, 4, 4, 5, 5) sts before BOR. BO 3 (3, 3, 4, 4, 5, 5) sts, remove BOR m, BO 3 (3, 3, 4, 4, 5, 5) sts. Place remaining stitches on scrap yarn or holders to be picked up later. 26 (32, 32, 32, 34, 36, 38) sts.

Repeat for the second sleeve.

Body

WWith smaller needles and MC, CO 98 (104, 110, 126, 140, 152, 160) sts. Join to work in the round, being careful not to twist the stitches. Place marker for BOR. Work in K1 P1 ribbing for 1.5 (1.5, 1.5, 2, 2, 2.5, 2.5)" / 3 (3, 3, 5, 5, 6, 6) cm.

Switch to larger needles. Work in St st until body measures 7 (8, 9, 10, 11, 12, 13)" / 18 (20, 23, 25, 28, 30, 33) cm from CO edge.

Last Rnd before Yoke: Knit to last 3 (3, 3, 4, 4, 5, 5) sts, BO 3 (3, 3, 4, 4, 5, 5) sts for underarm. 95 (101, 107, 122, 136, 147, 155) sts rem.

Yoke

Bind Off Rnd: K to 3 sts before BOR m, BO 3 (3, 3, 4, 4, 5, 5) sts, remove BOR m, BO 3 (3, 3, 4, 4, 5, 5) sts, K43 (46, 49, 55, 62, 66, 70), BO 6 (6, 6, 8, 8, 10, 10) sts K43 (46, 49, 55, 62, 66, 70). 86 (92, 98, 110, 124, 132, 140) sts.

Joining Rnd: Transfer the held sleeve stitches to LN and K26 (32, 32, 32, 34, 36, 38) sleeve sts, K43 (46, 49, 55, 62, 66, 70), transfer the second sleeve stitches to LN and K26 (32, 32, 32, 34, 36, 38) sleeve sts, K43 (46, 49, 55, 62, 66, 70). Place BOR M. 138 (156, 162, 174, 192, 204, 216) sts on needles.

Knit 0 (1, 1, 2, 5, 6, 9) rnds in MC.

Work Chart A (A, B, B, B, B, B).

Knit 1 (1, 1, 1, 1, 1, 1) rnd.

Decrease Rnd 1: *K3 (0, 0, 0, 0, 0, 0), (K5 (11, 7, 27, 6, 15, 7), K2tog) 9 (6, 9, 3, 12, 6, 12) times, K3 (0, 0, 0, 0, 0, 0); rep from * once more. 120 (144, 144, 168, 168, 192, 192) sts.

Work Chart C (C, D, D, D, D, D)

Knit 1 (1, 1, 1, 1, 1, 1) rnd.

Decrease Rnd 2: *K3 (4, 4, 5, 5, 6, 6) K2tog; repeat from * to the end of the rnd. 96 (120, 120, 144, 144, 168, 168) sts.

Work Chart E (E, E, E, E, E, E).

Decrease Rnd 3: *K0 (0, 0, 4, 4, 5, 5) K2tog; rep from * a total of 0 (0, 0, 24, 24, 24, 24) times. 96 (120, 120, 120, 120, 144, 144) sts.

Short Rows
These are worked to bring up the back of the neck for a more comfortable fit.

Set Up: Remove BOR m, K15 (19, 19, 19, 19, 22, 22) to the centre back, place m. This will also be your BOR m later.

Row 1 (RS): K24 (30, 30, 30, 30, 36, 36), W&T (see Special Techniques).
Row 2 (WS): Purl to m, sl m, P24 (30, 30, 30, 30, 36, 36), W&T.
Row 3: Knit to 6 sts before gap, W&T.

Row 4: Purl to 6 sts before gap, W&T.

Work Short Rows 3-4 a total of 1 (1, 1, 2, 2, 3, 3) time(s).

Next Round (RS): Knit to M, then knit 1 rnd, picking up and knitting all wraps together with the stitches they wrap.

Decrease Rnd 4: *K2 (2, 2, 4, 4, 4, 4), K2tog; rep from * to end. 72 (90, 90, 100, 100, 120, 120) sts rem.

Neck
Using smaller needles and MC, work in K1, P1 ribbing until neckline measures 0.75 (0.75, 1, 1, 1, 1.25, 1.25)"/ 2 (2, 2.5, 2.5, 2.5, 3, 3) cm. Bind off loosely in pattern.

Finishing
Seam together underarms. Weave in all ends. For best results, wet block your sweater in tepid water to relax the colourwork pattern.

CHART A

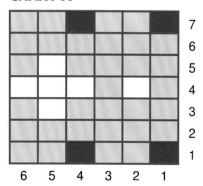

Row 1: K1 CC1, K2 MC, K1 CC1, K2 MC.
Row 2: Knit in MC.
Row 3: K4 MC, K1 CC2, K1 MC.
Row 4: K1 MC, K1 CC2, K1 MC, K3 CC2.
Row 5: K4 MC, K1 CC2, K1 MC.
Row 6: Knit in MC.
Row 7: K1 CC1, K2 MC, K1 CC1, K2 MC

CHART B

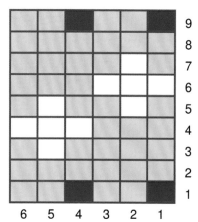

Row 1: K1 CC1, K2 MC, K1 CC1, K2 MC.
Row 2: Knit in MC.
Row 3: K4 MC, K1 CC2, K1 MC.
Row 4: K3 MC, K3 CC2.
Row 5: K1 MC, K1 CC2, K2 MC, K1 CC2, K1MC.
Row 6: K3 CC2, K3 MC.
Row 7: K1 MC, K1 CC2, K4 MC.
Row 8: Knit in MC.
Row 9: K1 CC1, K2 MC, K1 CC1, K2 MC.

CHART C

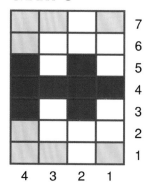

Row 1: K1 MC, K1 CC2, K2 MC.
Row 2: K3 CC2, K1 MC.
Row 3: K1 CC2, K1 CC1, K1 CC2, K1 CC1.
Row 4: Knit in CC1.
Row 5: K1 CC2, K1 CC1, K1 CC2, K1 CC1.
Row 6: K3 CC2, K1 MC.
Row 7: K1 MC, K1 CC2, K2 MC.

CHART D

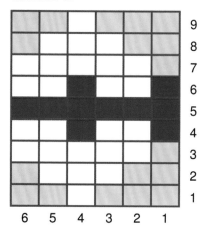

Row 1: K3 MC, K1 CC2, K2 MC.
Row 2: K2 MC, K3 CC2, K1 MC.
Row 3: K1 MC, K5 CC2.
Row 4: K1 CC1, K2 CC2, K1 CC1, K2 CC2.
Row 5: Knit in CC1.
Row 6: K1 CC1, K2 CC2, K1 CC1, K2 CC2.
Row 7: K1 MC, K5 CC2.
Row 8: K2 MC, K3 CC2, K1 MC.
Row 9: K3 MC, K1 CC2, K2 MC.

CHART E

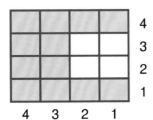

				4
				3
				2
				1
4	3	2	1	

Row 1: Knit in MC.

Row 2: K2 CC2, K2 MC.

Row 3: K2 CC2, K2 MC.

Row 4: Knit in MC.

CLOUdBERRY A cabled hat for everyone

A fancy yet functional hat for all seasons that uses large cables to create a soft, rippled texture inspired by the Newfoundland cloudberry, a.k.a. the bakeapple. Sizes range from newborn to adult, making it easy to create matching hats for the whole crew. The hat uses a DK-weight yarn to make it warm enough to withstand winter, but light enough for fall and spring.

SKILL LEVEL
Experienced beginner

Skills required:
knitting in the round, decreasing, cable knitting, ribbing

MATERIALS
Approximately 110 (120, 135, 145, 160, 180) yds / 101 (110, 123, 133, 146, 165) m DK-weight yarn.
Sample shown in Julie Asselin Leizu DK in col. "Biscotti," 260 yds / 238 m per 115 g skein.

4.0 mm (US 6) needles for knitting in the round
4.5 mm (US 7) needles for knitting in the round
Or size required to obtain gauge

Tapestry needle
Cable needle
Optional: Faux fur pompom

GAUGE
24 sts and 32 rnds = 4" / 10 cm
In cable pattern with 4.5 mm (US 7) needles

SIZES
Baby (Toddler, Child, Adult Small, Adult Medium, Adult Large)
Finished circumference: 14 (16, 18, 20, 22, 24)" / 36 (41, 46, 51, 56, 61) cm

INSTRUCTIONS

With 4.0 mm (US 6) needles CO 84 (96, 108, 120, 132, 144) sts and join to work in the rnd, being careful not to twist the stitches.

Work 8 (10, 10, 12, 12, 12) rnds in twisted ribbing as follows: *K1 TBL, P1; rep from * to end of rnd.

Body

Change to 4.5 mm (US 7) needles. Begin the cable pattern using Chart A. This 12-stitch repeat is worked 7 (8, 9, 10, 11, 12) times across the rnd.

Repeat Rnds 1–12 of Chart A until the hat measures approximately 2" / 5 cm shorter than desired length, ending after Rnd 6 or 12.

Decreases

The top of the hat is decreased using Decrease Charts A and B. If you've ended with Rnd 6, continue to Decrease Chart A. If you've ended with Rnd 12, continue to Decrease Chart B. These charts are worked 7 (8, 9, 10, 11, 12) times across the rnd.

Work Rnds 1–16 of Decrease Chart. 7 (8, 9, 10, 11, 12) sts rem.

Finishing

Cut yarn, leaving a 6" / 15 cm tail. Thread tail through remaining stitches and pull to close. Secure the tail. Weave in all ends. Block for best results. Optional: Add faux fur pompom to top of hat.

CHARTS

Charts are 12-stitch repeats worked 7 (8, 9, 10, 11, 12) times across the body of the hat.

CHART A

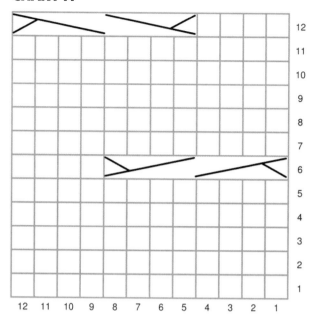

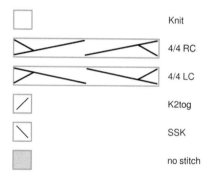

	Knit
	4/4 RC
	4/4 LC
/	K2tog
\	SSK
	no stitch

Row 1: K12.
Row 2: K12.
Row 3: K12.
Row 4: K12.
Row 5: K12.
Row 6: 4/4 RC, K4.
Row 7: K12.
Row 8: K12.
Row 9: K12.
Row 10: K12.
Row 11: K12.
Row 12: K4, 4/4 LC.

CLOUDBERRY DECREASE

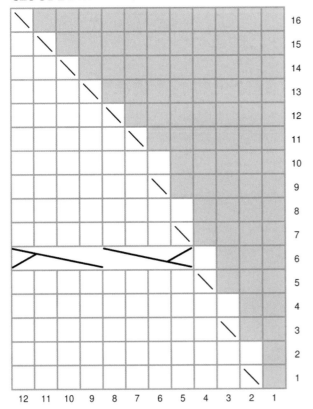

DECREASE

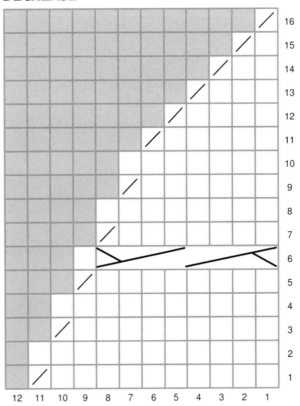

CHART A

Row 1: SSK, K10.

Row 2: K11.

Row 3: SSK, K9.

Row 4: K10.

Row 5: SSK, K8.

Row 6: K1, (4/4 LC).

Row 7: SSK, K7.

Row 8: K8.

Row 9: SSK, K6.

Row 10: K7.

Row 11: SSK, K5.

Row 12: SSK, K4.

Row 13: SSK, K3.

Row 14: SSK, K2.

Row 15: SSK, K.

Row 16: SSK.

CHART B

Row 1: K10, K2tog.

Row 2: K11.

Row 3: K9, K2tog.

Row 4: K10.

Row 5: K8, K2tog.

Row 6: 4/4 RC, K1.

Row 7: K7, K2tog.

Row 8: K8.

Row 9: K6, K2tog.

Row 10: K7, no stitch.

Row 11: K5, K2tog.

Row 12: K4, K2tog.

Row 13: K3, K2tog 8.

Row 14: K2, K2tog.

Row 15: K, K2tog.

Row 16: K2tog.

FLURRIES Thrummed mittens

Thrummed mittens are a staple in Newfoundland knitting. In the thrumming technique, scraps of unspun wool roving are knit into the fabric to create a soft and fuzzy lining, with little puffs of fuzz showing on the outside. While these are super cute, they also serve the important purpose of keeping little fingers warm during cold, damp winters.

SKILL LEVEL
Experienced beginner

Skills required:
knitting in the round, increasing, decreasing, thrumming, picking up stitches

MATERIALS
Approximately 55 (61, 67, 74, 81, 89) yds / 50 (56, 61, 68, 74, 81) m of bulky-weight yarn, 16 (18, 20, 22, 25, 28) g of wool roving. Sample shown in Cascade Eco col. 3103 "Legion Blue," 478 yds / 437 m per 250 g skein; thrums made with Fleece Artist Merino, 50 g per hank.

4.5 mm (US 7) needles for knitting in the round
5.0 mm (US 8) needles for knitting in the round
Or size required to obtain gauge

Tapestry needle
Stitch marker

GAUGE
20 sts and 28 rnds = 4" / 10 cm
In stockinette stitch with 5.0 mm (US 8) needles

SIZES
Baby (Toddler, Child, Adult Small, Adult Medium, Adult Large)
Finished circumference: 4.75 (5.5, 6.5, 7.25, 8, 8.75)" / 12 (14, 16.5, 18.5, 20.5, 22) cm

INSTRUCTIONS

With 4.5 mm (US 7) needles, CO 24 (28, 32, 36, 40, 44) sts. Join to work in the rnd and place BOR M. Work 10 (10, 12, 12, 14, 14) rnds in K2, P2 ribbing.

Hand

Change to 5.0 mm (US 8) needles.

Increase Rnd: *K6 (7, 8, 9, 10, 11), M1; rep from * to end of rnd. 28 (32, 36, 40, 44, 48) sts.

Begin Thrumming

Rnd 1–2: Knit.

Rnd 3: *K3, place thrum (see Special Techniques); rep from * to end of rnd.

Rnds 4–7: Knit.

Rnd 8: *K1, place thrum, K2; rep from * to end of rnd.

Rnds 9–10: Knit.

Work Rnds 1–10 1 (1, 1, 2, 2, 3) time(s). Then, work rnds -- (--, 1–5, --, 1–5, --) once more.

Thumb Insert

Note: There is no thumb for the baby size!

Left Thumb: K1, Place -- (5, 6, 7, 8, 8) sts on a stitch holder/scrap yarn, CO -- (5, 6, 7, 8, 8) sts using the backward loop method (see Special Techniques), K to end of rnd.

Right Thumb: K to last 1 (6, 7, 8, 9, 9) st(s), place -- (5, 6, 7, 8, 8) sts on a stitch holder/scrap yarn, CO -- (5, 6, 7, 8, 8) sts using the backward loop method, K1.

Continue working the hand as follows:

Work Rnds -- (--, 6–10, --, 6–10, --), work Rnds 1–10 1 (1, 2, 2, 3, 3) time(s). Finally work Rnds -- (1–5, --, 1–5, --, 1–5) or until hand measures 1" / 2.5 cm shorter than desired length, ending after Rnd 5 or 10.

Top

For Baby (Child, Adult Medium) or ended after Rnd 10

Rnd 1: *SSK, K2; rep from * to end of rnd. 21 (27, 33) sts rem.

Rnd 2: Knit.

Rnd 3: *K2 place thrum; rep from * to end of rnd.

Rnd 4: Knit.

Rnd 5: *SSK, K1; rep to end of rnd. 14 (18, 22) sts rem.

Rnd 6: SSK around. 7 (9, 11) sts rem.

Rnd 7: *SSK around, K1 (1, 1). 4 (5, 6) sts rem.

For Toddler (Adult Small, Adult Large) or ended after Rnd 5

Rnd 1: *K2, K2tog; rep from * to end of rnd. 24 (30, 36) sts rem.

Rnd 2: Knit.

Rnd 3: *K1, place thrum, K1; rep from * to end of rnd.

Rnd 4: Knit.

Rnd 5: *K1, K2tog; rep from * to end of rnd. 16 (20, 24) sts rem.

Rnd 6: K2tog around. 8 (10, 12) rem.

Rnd 7: K2tog around. 4 (5, 6) sts rem.

Cut yarn, leaving a 6" / 15 cm tail. Thread through the live stitches and pull tightly to close.

Thumb

Place -- (5, 6, 7, 8, 8) held sts onto 4.5 mm (US 7) needles. Join yarn and work across the -- (5, 6, 7, 8, 8) sts, PU 1 in the gap, PU -- (5, 6, 7, 8, 8) sts from CO sts, PU 1 in the gap. -- (12, 14, 16, 18, 18) sts total. Join to work in the round.

Work in St st until thumb measures approximately 1.5 (1.75, 2, 2.25, 2.75)" / 4 (4.5, 5, 6, 7) cm, or until it reaches the desired length.

Dec Rnd 1: K2tog around. 6 (7, 8, 9, 9) sts rem.
Dec Rnd 2: *K2tog around, K -- (--, 1, --, 1, 1). -- (3, 4, 4, 4, 4) sts rem.

Cut yarn, leaving a 6" / 15 cm tail. Thread through the live stitches and pull tightly to close.

Finishing

Weave in all ends. Turn the mitten inside out and tug on thrums gently to ensure that they are secured. Blocking is not necessary for these mittens.

WOOdStOVe *A pair of overalls*

Stretchy and sweet, these overalls are perfect no matter the time of year. Functionally, they make a great layering outfit while also being warm, and grow-with-me cuffs are included to have more time before sizing up. The cables that run along the length of the legs and the straps accent the stockinette stitch body, giving them a bit of traditional Newfoundland flair.

SKILL LEVEL
Experienced beginner

Skills required: knitting in the round, increasing, decreasing, thrumming, picking up stitches

MATERIALS
Approximately 306 (340, 375, 412, 453, 498, 548) yds / 280 (311, 343, 377, 414, 455, 501) m DK-weight yarn. Sample shown in Biscotte Yarns DK Pure, col. "Chocolat," 260 yds / 238 m per 115 g skein.

4.0 mm (US 6) needles for knitting in the round
4.5 mm (US 7) needles for knitting in the round
Or size required to obtain gauge

Tapestry needle
Stitch markers (2)

GAUGE
22 sts and 30 rnds = 4" / 10 cm
In stockinette stitch with larger needles

SIZES
0–6 mo (6–12 mo, 1–2, 2–4, 4–6, 6–8, 8–10)
Finished waist measurements: 18 (18.5, 20, 21, 22, 22.5, 23.5)" / 46 (47, 51, 53, 56, 57, 60) cm
Meant to be worn with 0–1.5" of positive ease

INSTRUCTIONS

Cuff

Using 4.0 mm (US 6) needles, CO 32 (36, 40, 44, 48, 52, 56) sts. Join to knit in the rnd, being careful not to twist the sts. Work in K1, P1 ribbing for 30 (30, 30, 30, 40, 40, 40) rnds.

Legs

Switch to 4.5 mm (US 7) needles.

Set-up Rnd: [K5 (6, 7, 8, 9, 10, 11), M1] twice, PM, P2, K4, M1, K4, P2, PM, [K5 (6, 7, 8, 9, 10, 11), M1] twice. 37 (41, 45, 49, 53, 57, 61) sts.

Rnds 1–7: K to M, Sl M, insert Leg Chart Row, K to end.

Rnd 8: K1, M1L, K to M, Sl M, insert Leg Chart Row, Sl M, K to last stitch, M1R, K1.

Repeat Rnds 1–8 until you have 49 (53, 59, 65, 71, 77, 85) sts on the needles. Continue working even until leg measures 9 (10.5, 13.5, 16.5, 18, 22, 26)" / 23 (37, 34, 42, 46, 56, 66) cm, or until the leg reaches the desired length. Place stitches on a spare pair of needles/scrap yarn and repeat these instructions for the second leg.

Body

Joining Rnd: Work across 49 (53, 59, 65, 71, 77, 85) leg sts on needle, CO 6 (6 7, 8, 9, 10, 10) using the backward-loop method, place stitches for other leg on needle, work across 49 (53, 59, 65, 71, 77, 85) leg sts, CO 6 (6 7, 8, 9, 10, 10) using the backward-loop method, place BOR M. This is the back of the overalls. 110 (118, 132, 146, 160, 174, 190) sts.

Work evenly, maintaining the cable stitch pattern along the sides until the body measures 6.5 (7, 7.75, 8.5, 9.5, 10.25, 11.25)" / 16.5, 18, 19.5, 21.5, 24, 26, 28.5) cm from joining rnd or until body reaches approximately 4" / 10 cm shorter than the desired height of the bib.

Divide for front and back: K to M, remove M, BO 13, remove M, K to next M, remove M, BO 13, remove M. Place the stitches for the front on a spare needle/stitch holder, continue to work the back. 42 (46, 53, 60, 67, 74, 82) sts for front and back each.

Back

Row 1 (RS): K1, SSK, K to last 3 sts, K2tog, K1.
Row 2 (WS): K1, P to last stitch, K1.

Repeat these two rows until 20 (22, 23, 26, 29, 32, 36) sts remain, ending after a WS row. Do not cut yarn.

Divide for straps (RS): K10 (10, 10, 12, 14, 16, 16), BO 0 (2, 3, 2, 1, 0, 4), K10 (10, 10, 12, 14, 16, 16). Place the first 10 (10, 10, 12, 14, 16, 16) sts on holder.
Next Row (WS): K2, P6 (6, 6, 9, 9, 12, 12), K2.

Continue working the strap as follows:
Row 1 (RS): K1 (1, 1, 2, 3, 4, 4), work Row 1 of Strap Chart, K1 (1, 1, 2, 3, 4, 4).
Row 2 (WS): K1 (1, 1, 2, 3, 4, 4), work Row 2 of Strap Chart, K1 (1, 1, 2, 3, 4, 4).

Continue working in this manner, working through Rows 1–8 of the chart pattern, and repeating until the strap measures approximately 8 (9, 10, 11, 12, 13, 14.5)" / 20.5 (23, 25.5, 28, 30.5, 33, 37) cm from divide, ending after a WS row.

Dec Row 1 (RS): K1 (1, 1, 2, 3, 4, 4), SSK, K to last 3 (3, 3, 4, 5, 6, 6) sts, K2tog, K1 (1, 1, 2, 3, 4, 4). 8 (8, 8, 10, 12, 14, 14) sts rem.

Next Row (WS): K1 (1, 1, 2, 3, 4, 4), P to last K1 (1, 1, 2, 3, 4, 4) st(s), K1 (1, 1, 2, 3, 4, 4).

Dec Row 2: As Dec Row 1. 6 (6, 6, 8, 10, 12, 12) sts rem.

BO kwise. Place held strap sts to working needle and repeat instructions for second strap.

Front

Place 42 (46, 53, 60, 67, 74, 82) held sts on working needles.

Row 1 (RS): K1, SSK, K to last 3 sts, K2tog, K1.
Row 2 (WS): K1, P to last stitch, K1.

Repeat these two rows until 32 (36, 41, 46, 49, 58, 60) sts remain, ending after a RS row.

Work 3 (3, 3, 5, 5, 7, 7) rows even in garter stitch.

Buttonhole Row (RS): K3, K2tog, YO, K to last 5 sts, YO, K2tog, K3.

Work 3 (3, 3, 5, 5, 7, 7) rows even in garter stitch. BO loosely kwise on the WS.

Finishing

Weave in all ends. Seam together front and back CO sts from the joining rnd. Blocking is recommended to relax the cable patterns. Attach a button to the end of each strap.

CHARTS

Leg Chart

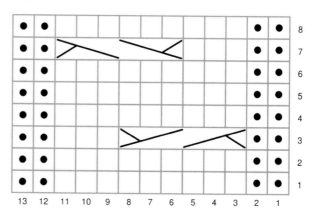

13 12 11 10 9 8 7 6 5 4 3 2 1

| | Knit | ● | Purl |

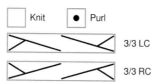

3/3 LC

3/3 RC

Rnds 1–2: P2, K9, P2.
Rnd 3: P2, 3/3 RC, K3, P2.
Rnds 4–6: P2, K9, P2.
Rnd 7: P2, K3, 3/3 LC, P2.
Rnd 8: P2, K9, P2.

Strap Chart

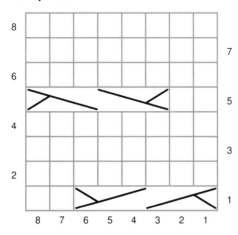

Row 1 (RS): 3/3 RC, K2.

Row 2 (WS): Purl.

Row 3: Knit.

Row 4: Purl.

Row 5: K2, 3/3 LC.

Row 6: Purl.

Row 7: Knit.

Row 8: Purl.

WISP *A hooded poncho*

Little Red Riding Hood meets the east coast. Great for the rain, drizzle, and fog, this hooded poncho is a must-have for little explorers! The hood is functional, giving kids the option to get outside even when the sun hides away. The cable along the bottom edge is a nod to the Celtic heritage and adds visual interest as well as a traditional element to this whimsical knit.

SKILL LEVEL
Experienced beginner

Skills required:
knitting in the round, increasing, decreasing, cable knitting

MATERIALS
Approximately 456 (495, 550, 605, 665, 732, 805) yds / 417 (453, 503, 553, 608, 669, 736) m worsted-weight yarn. Sample shown in Cascade 220 col. 9448 "Olive Heather" 220 yds / 201 m per 100 g skein.

5.0 mm (US 8) needles for knitting in the round
5.0 mm (US 8) needles for knitting flat
6.0 mm (US 10) needles for knitting flat
6.0 mm (US 10) DPN (to work cable edge)
Or size required to obtain gauge

Tapestry needle
Stitch markers

GAUGE
17 sts and 24 rows = 4" / 10 cm
In stockinette stitch with 5.0 mm (US 8) needles

SIZES
0–6 mo (6–12 mo, 1–2, 2–4, 4–6, 6–8, 8–10)
Finished hem circumference: 37.5 (41.5, 45, 51, 56.5, 62, 68)" / 95 (105, 114, 130, 144, 157, 173) cm
Meant to fit loosely

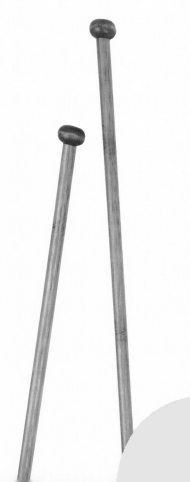

INSTRUCTIONS

Hood

With 5.0 mm (US 8) needles, CO 54 (60, 68, 76, 88, 96, 106) sts using the long-tail CO (see Special Techniques). PM at the centre of the CO sts. Work 4 rows in St st.

Row 1 (RS): K to 4 sts before M, K2tog, K2, Sl M, K2, SSK, K to end. 52 (58, 66, 74, 86, 94, 104) sts rem.
Row 2 (WS): Purl.
Row 3: Knit.
Row 4: Purl.

Repeat Rows 1–4 7 (7, 8, 8, 9, 9, 10) more times. 38 (44, 50, 58, 68, 76, 84) sts. Work even in St st until hood measures 8 (9, 10, 11, 12, 13, 14.5)" / 20.5 (23, 25.5, 28, 30.5, 33, 37) cm.

Dec Row: K to 6 sts before M, K2tog three times, Sl M, K2tog three times, K to end. 32 (38, 44, 52, 62, 70, 78) sts rem.

Continue working in St st until hood measures 9 (10, 12, 13, 14, 15, 16.5)" / 23 (25.5, 30.5, 33, 35.5, 38, 42) cm.

Increases: Set Up: K6 (7, 8, 10, 13, 15, 17), PM, K10 (12, 14, 16, 18, 20, 22), Sl M, K10 (12, 14, 16, 18, 20, 22), PM, K6 (7, 8, 10, 13, 15, 17).

Work the WS in patt.

Row 1 (RS): K1 (1, 1, 2, 4, 5, 6), M1P, K5 (6, 7, 8, 9, 10, 11), M1P, Sl M, [K5 (6, 7, 8, 9, 10, 11) M1P] twice, Sl M, [K5 (6, 7, 8, 9, 10, 11) M1P] twice, Sl M, K5 (6, 7, 8, 9, 10, 11), M1P, K1 (1, 1, 2, 4, 5, 6). 39 (45, 51, 59, 69, 77, 85) sts.

Row 2 (WS): Work across the WS in patt.

Row 3: K1, M1L, work in patt to last stitch, M1R, K1 (2 sts inc).

Row 4: Work across the WS in patt.

Row 5: K1, M1L, *work in patt to 2 sts before M, M1R, K1, P1, Sl M, K1, M1L; rep from * twice more, work in patt to last stitch, M1R, K1 (8 sts inc).

Row 6: Work across the WS in patt.

Continue working Rows 3–6 until there are 17 (21, 22, 24, 27, 29, 31) sts for the right front, 18 (22, 24, 26, 28, 30, 32) sts between each of the markers, and 16 (20, 21, 23, 26, 28, 30) sts for the left front, ending after Row 3 or 5. 69 (85, 91, 99, 109, 117, 125) sts.

Joining to work in the rnd

With the RS facing, CO 2 (2, 3, 3, 2, 2, 2) using the backward-loop method (see Special Techniques). Turn work (WS now facing), P CO st(s), work in patt to end of row, CO 1 (1, 2, 2, 1, 1, 1). Turn work (RS now facing), work in patt to 1 st before end of row, P1, place BOR M, join to work in the rnd. 72 (88, 96, 104, 112, 120, 128) sts.

Cable Edge

The cabled edge is created by casting on stitches and knitting vertically along the hem. To make this process easier, a spare 6.0 mm (US 10) needle or DPN is recommended.

Set Up: With the RS facing, remove BOR M, K1 from LN. Using the cable CO method (see Special Techniques), cast on 22 sts. Do not turn your work.

Row 1 (RS): K3, P1, K2, P4, K4, P4, K2, P1, SSK kwise (this will be 1 st from the CO sts and 1 from the existing hem). Turn.
Row 2 (WS): Sl 1 from the RN to the LN, P2tog TBL, work to the end of the row in patt.
Row 3: K3, work Row 1 of Chart A, SSK kwise.
Row 4: Sl 1 from the RN to the LN, P2tog TBL, work to the end of the row in patt.

Repeat Rows 3–4, working through Rows 1–8 of the chart pattern until all hem sts have been worked. BO loosely. Cut yarn, leaving a 6" / 15 cm tail and use the horizontal seaming method (see Special Techniques) to seam the ends together.

Hood Front

Before starting the ribbing, seam the hood together using the horizontal seaming method.

With the RS facing and using 6.0 mm (US 10) needles for knitting flat, start at the corner of the V-neck and pick up and knit 2 sts for every 3 rows along the edge of the hood, approximately 87 (97, 115, 125, 135, 145, 159) sts.

Continue working in the rnd in patt and increase every 4th rnd as follows:

Inc Rnd: K1, M1L, *work in patt to 2 sts before M, M1R, K1, P1, Sl M, K1, M1L; rep from * twice more, K to last 2 sts, M1R, K1, P1 (8 sts inc).

Work until you have 160 (176, 192, 216, 240, 264, 288) sts on the needle.

Switch to 6.0 mm (US 10) needles, work one more rnd in patt.

Row 1 (WS): *P1, K1; rep from * to last stitch, P1.

Row 2 (RS): Work in rib patt until 5 sts rem, W&T.

Row 3: Work in rib patt until 5 sts rem, W&T.

Row 4: Work in rib patt until there are 5 sts left before the wrap, W&T.

Row 5: Work in rib patt until there are 5 sts left before the wrap, W&T.

Rep Rows 4–5 a total of 9 (9, 11, 11, 13, 13) times.

Pick Up Row 1: After turning your work, work in rib pattern to the end of the row, picking up the wraps and knitting them together with their corresponding stitch. Turn.

Pick Up Row 2: Work in rib pattern to the end of the row, picking up the wraps and knitting them together with their corresponding stitch.

Finishing

Bind off loosely in pattern. Close the gap between the hood stitch at the bottom of the V-neck. Weave in all ends and block to relax cable pattern and allow for a better drape.

CHART

Row 1 (RS): P1, [2/2 LPC, 2/2 RPC] twice, P1.

Row 2 (WS): K3, P4, K4, P4, K3.

Row 3: P3, 2/2 RC, P4, 2/2 RC, P3.

Row 4: K3, P4, K4, P4, K3.

Row 5: P1, [2/2 RPC, 2/2 LPC] twice, P1.

Row 6: K1, P2, K4, P4, K4, P2, K1.

Row 7: P1, K2, P4, 2/2 LC, P4, K2, P1.

Row 8: K1, P2, K4, P4, K4, P2, K1.

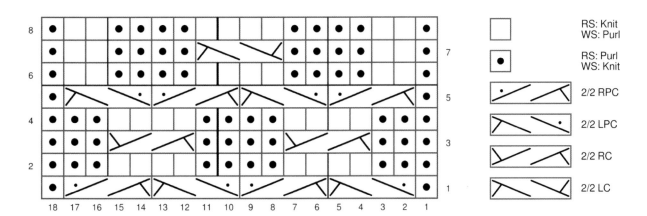

DORY A cabled sweater

A classic design rooted deep in Newfoundland knitting tradition. Cabled fisherman-knit sweaters are renowned for their beautiful knots, twists, and ropes and this sweater follows suit with a variety of cables along the front and back. To suit the needs of kids, this sweater features a wider neck and plain sleeves to keep it feeling light and comfortable during play.

SKILL LEVEL
Intermediate

Skills required:
working in the round, cable knitting, picking up stitches, decreasing, grafting

MATERIALS
Approximately 393 (437, 480, 529, 581, 640, 703) yds / 359 (400, 439, 484, 531, 585, 643) m DK-weight yarn.
Sample shown in Biscotte Yarns DK Pure, col. "Klimt," 260 yds / 238 m per 115 g skein.

4.0 mm (US 6) needles for knitting flat and in the round
4.5 mm (US 7) needles for knitting flat and in the round
Or size required to obtain gauge

Tapestry needle
Stitch marker

GAUGE
26 sts and 32 rnds = 4" / 10 cm
In cable pattern, worked in the round with 4.5 mm (US 7) needles, after blocking

SIZES
Sizes: 0–6 mo (6–12 mo, 1–2, 2–4, 4–6, 6–8, 8–10)
Finished chest measurement: 17 (18, 20, 23, 25, 26.5, 28)" / 43 (46, 51, 58, 64, 67, 71) cm
Garment is meant to be fitted on the chest with 0–2" / 0–5 cm of positive ease

INSTRUCTIONS

Front

Using smaller needles, CO 54 (58, 64, 74, 80, 86, 90). Work in K1, P1 ribbing for 1.5 (1.5, 1.5, 2, 2, 2.5, 2.5)" / 4 (4, 4, 5, 5, 6, 6) cm, ending after a RS row.

Switch to larger needles and work set up row for size as indicated below:

Size 0–6 mo (6–12 mo, 1–2): P1 (3, 6), K4, P5, K4, P4, K1, P16, K1, P4, K4, P5, K4, P1 (3, 6).
Size 2–4 (4–6): P4 (7), K1, P6, K4, P5, K4, P4, K1, P16, K1, P4, K4, P5, K4, P6, K1, P4 (7).
Size 6–8 (8–10): P5 (7), K1, P4, K1, P6, K4, P5, K4, P4, K1, P16, K1, P4, K4, P5, K4, P6, K1, P4, K1, P5 (7).

Next begin working the cables as indicated below, starting with Row 1 of the cable charts:

Size 0–6 mo (6–12 mo, 1–2)
Row 1 (RS): K1 (3, 6), P1, Chart C, P1, Chart A, P1, Chart D, P1, Chart A, P1, Chart C, P1, K1 (3, 6).
Row 2 (WS): P1 (3, 6), K1, Chart C, K1, Chart A, K1, Chart D, K1, Chart A, K1, Chart C, K1, P1 (3, 6).

Size 2–4 (4–6)
Row 1 (RS): K4 (7), P1, Chart B, P1, Chart C, P1, Chart A, P1, Chart D, P1, Chart A, P1, Chart C, P1, Chart B, P1, K4 (7).
Row 2 (WS): P4 (7), K1, Chart B, K1, Chart C, K1, Chart A, K1, Chart D, K1, Chart A, K1, Chart C, K1, Chart B, K1, P4 (7).

Size 6–8 (8–10)
Row 1 (RS): K5 (7), P1, Chart A, P1, Chart B, P1, Chart C, P1, Chart A, P1, Chart D, P1, Chart A, P1, Chart C, P1, Chart B, P1, Chart A, P1, K5 (7).
Row 2 (WS): P5 (7), K1, Chart A, K1, Chart B, K1, Chart C, K1, Chart A, K1, Chart D, K1, Chart A, K1, Chart C, K1, Chart B, K1, Chart A, K1, P5 (7).

Repeat charts until body measures 8.75 (10, 11.25, 12.5, 13.75, 15, 16.5)" / 22 (25.5, 28.5, 31, 35, 38, 42) cm from CO edge, or until front reaches desired length to the beginning of the collar.

Front Neck Shaping

BO Row (RS): Work 19 (20, 22, 27, 29, 31, 32) sts in patt, BO 16 (18, 20, 20, 22, 24, 26), work 19 (20, 22, 27, 29, 31, 32) sts in patt.
Next Row (WS): Work 19 (20, 22, 27, 29, 31, 32) sts for right strap in patt, place the 19 (20, 22, 27, 29, 31, 32) sts for the left strap on stitch holder/ scrap yarn.

Right Strap Shaping

BO Row 1 (RS): BO 3 sts kwise, work to end of row in patt. 16 (17, 19, 24, 26, 28, 29) sts rem.
Next Row (WS): Work across in patt.
Repeat these rows 0 (0, 0, 0, 0, 1, 1) more time(s). 16 (17, 19, 24, 26, 25, 26) sts rem.

BO Row 2: BO 2 sts kwise, work to end of row in patt. 14 (15, 17, 22, 24, 23, 24) sts rem.

Next Row: Work across in patt.

Repeat these rows 1 (1, 1, 1, 2, 2, 2) more time(s). 12 (13, 15, 20, 20, 19, 20) sts rem.

BO Row 3: BO 1 st kwise, work to end of row in patt. 11 (12, 14, 19, 19, 18, 19) sts rem.

Next Row: Work across in patt.

Continue working even in patt until the piece measures 10.5 (12, 13.5, 15, 16.5, 18, 19.5)" / 27 (30, 34, 38, 42, 46, 50) cm from the CO edge,

ending after a RS row. Cut yarn, leaving a 6" / 15 cm tail. Place live sts on stitch holder / scrap yarn to be grafted to the back stitches.

Left Strap Shaping

Place 19 (20, 22, 27, 29, 31, 32) held sts on working needles. Join yarn to begin working a WS row.

BO Row 1 (WS): BO 3 sts pwise, work to end of row in patt. 16 (17, 19, 24, 26, 28, 29) sts rem.

Next Row (RS): Work across row in patt.

Repeat these two rows 0 (0, 0, 0, 0, 1, 1) more time(s). 16 (17, 19, 24, 26, 25, 26) sts rem.

BO Row 2: BO 2 sts pwise, work to end of row in patt. 14 (15, 17, 22, 24, 23, 24) sts rem.

Next Row: Work across in patt.

Repeat these two rows 1 (1, 1, 1, 2, 2, 2) more time(s). 12 (13, 15, 20, 20, 19, 20) sts rem.

BO Row 3: BO 1 st pwise, work to end of row in patt. 11 (12, 14, 19, 19, 18, 19) sts rem.

Next Row: Work across in patt.

Continue working even in patt until the piece measures 10.5 (12, 13.5, 15, 16.5, 18, 19.5)" / 27 (30, 34, 38, 42, 46, 50) cm from the CO edge, ending after a RS row. Cut yarn, leaving a 6" / 15 cm tail. Place live sts on stitch holder/scrap yarn to be grafted to the back stitches.

Back

Repeat instructions for front, working the cable charts until the piece measures 10.25 (11.75, 13.25, 14.75, 16.25, 17.75, 19.25)" / 26 (30, 33.5, 37.5, 41.5, 45, 49) cm from the CO edge, or until the piece measures 0.25" / 0.5 cm shorter than desired length to back of neck.

BO Row (RS): Work 11 (12, 14, 19, 19, 18, 19) sts in patt, BO 32 (34, 36, 36, 42, 50, 52) sts, work 11 (12, 14, 19, 19, 18, 19) sts in patt.

WS: Work 11 (12, 14, 19, 19, 18, 19) sts for left strap in patt, place the 11 (12, 14, 19, 19, 18, 19) sts for the right strap on stitch holder/scrap yarn.

Left Strap

Continue working even in patt until the piece measures 10.5 (12, 13.5, 15, 16.5, 18, 19.5)" / 27

(30, 34, 38, 42, 46, 50) cm from the CO edge, ending after a RS row. Cut yarn, leaving a 6" / 15 cm tail. Place live sts on holder to be grafted to the back stitches.

Right Strap

Place 11 (12, 14, 19, 19, 18, 19) held sts on working needles. Join yarn to begin working a WS row. Continue working even in patt until the piece measures 10.5 (12, 13.5, 15, 16.5, 18, 19.5)" / 27 (30, 34, 38, 42, 46, 50) cm from the CO edge, ending after a RS row. Cut yarn, leaving a 6" / 15 cm tail. Place live sts on stitch holder/scrap yarn to be grafted to the back stitches.

Joining Front and Back

The front and back straps are joined together using the kitchener stitch. Place the front and back stitches on separate needles, hold them with the WS sides together and use the kitchener stitch to graft the stitches together. Rep for the other side. Seam the sides of the sweater using the mattress stitch, leaving a 3.5 (4, 4.5, 5, 5.5, 6, 6.5)" / 9 (10, 11, 13, 14, 15, 17) cm gap at the top of each side for the sleeves.

NECKLINE

Using smaller needles, start on the left shoulder and pick up and knit 56 (62, 68, 76, 84, 92, 100) sts around the neckline. Work in K1, P1 ribbing for 1 (1, 1.5, 1.5, 2, 2, 2)" / 2.5, 2.5, 3, 3, 5, 5, 5) cm. BO loosely in pattern; cut yarn, leaving a 6" / 15 cm tail.

SLEEVES

Using smaller needles, start at theunderarm, pick up and knit 42 (48, 54, 60, 66, 72, 78) sts around the opening for the sleeve. Place BOR M and join to work in the round.

Rnds 1–4: Knit
Rnd 5: K1, SSK, K to 3 sts before BOR, K2tog, K1 (2 sts dec).
Repeat Rnds 1–5 5 (5, 6, 7, 8, 9, 11) more times. 30 (36, 40, 44, 48, 52, 54) sts rem.

Work in St st until sleeve measures 5 (6, 7, 8.5, 9.5, 10, 11)" / 13 (15, 18, 22, 24, 25, 28) cm from underarm, or until arm measures 1.5 (1.5, 1.5, 2, 2, 2.5, 2.5)" / 3 (3, 3, 5, 5, 6, 6) cm shorter than desired length.

Switch to smaller needles and work in K1, P1 ribbing for 1.5 (1.5, 1.5, 2, 2, 2.5, 2.5)" / 3 (3, 3, 5, 5, 6, 6) cm. BO loosely in pattern. Cut yarn, leaving a 6" / 15 cm tail. Repeat for second arm.

Finishing

Weave in all ends. Blocking is recommended to relax and open cable patterning. For best results, use blocking wires to keep the edges straight.

CHART A

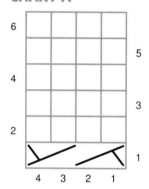

Row 1 (RS): 2/2 RC.

Row 2 (and all WS rows): P4.

Row 3: K4.

Row 5: K4.

CHART B

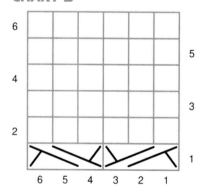

Row 1 (RS): 1/2 RC, 1/2 LC.

Row 2 (and all WS rows): P6.

Row 3: K6.

Row 5: K6.

CHART C

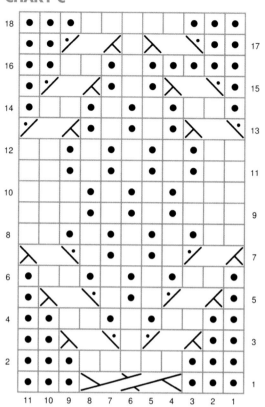

Row 1: P3, 2/1/2 RC, P3.

Row 2: K3, P5, K3.

Row 3: P2, 2/1 RPC, K1, 2/1 LPC, P2.

Row 4: K2, P2, K1, P1, K1, P2, K2.

Row 5: P1, 2/1 RPC, K1, P1, K1, 2/1 LPC, P1.

Row 6: K1, P2, (K1, P1) twice, K1, P2, K1.

Row 7: 2/1 RPC, (K1, P1) twice K1, 2/1 LPC1.

Row 8: P2, K1, (P1, K1) twice, P1, K1, P2.

Row 9: K3, (P1, K1) twice, P1, K3.

Row 10: P3, (K1, P1) twice, K1, P3.

Row 11: K2, (P1, K1) three times, P1, K2.

Row 12: P2, (K1, P1) three times, K1, P2.

Row 13: 2/1 LPC, (P1, K1) twice, P1, 2/1 RPC.

Row 14: K1, P2, (K1, P1) twice, K1, P2, K1.

Row 15: P1, 2/1 LPC, P1, K1, P1, 2/1 RPC, P1.

Row 16: K2, P2, K1, P1, K5.

Row 17: P2, 2/1 LPC, K1, 2/1 RPC, P2.

Row 18: K3, P5, K3.

CHART D

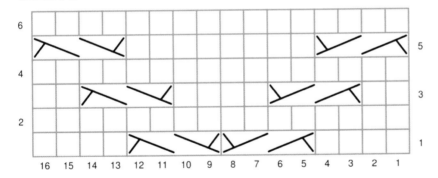

Row 1: K4, 2/2 RC, 2/2 LC, K4.

Row 2: P16.

Row 3: K2, 2/2 RC, K4, 2/2 LC, K2.

Row 4: P16.

Row 5: 2/2 RC, K8, 2/2 LC.

Row 6: P16.

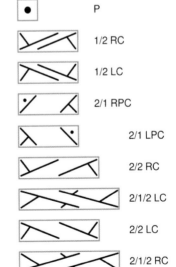

☐	K
●	P
	1/2 RC
	1/2 LC
	2/1 RPC
	2/1 LPC
	2/2 RC
	2/1/2 LC
	2/2 LC
	2/1/2 RC

TidePOOL Newfoundland bubble mittens

Designed for all ages, these mittens are inspired by the pools left behind when the tide goes out, a favourite place to explore ocean life. The "bubble" texture is created through alternating slipped stitch textures using two colours of yarn. In particular, these are a great option for using variegated and speckled yarns, as the texture helps break up the colours.

SKILL LEVEL
Experienced beginner

Skills required:
knitting in the round, decreasing, slipped stitches, picking up stitches

MATERIALS
Approximately 140 (154, 172, 191, 210) yds / 128 (141, 157, 175, 192) m worsted-weight yarn; 64 (71, 79, 88, 96) yds / 59 (65, 72, 80, 88) m MC, 75 (83, 92, 103, 113) yds / 69 (76, 84, 94, 103) m CC. Samples shown in Knit Picks Swish Worsted, 110 yds / 100 m per 50 g ball, in "Rainforest Heather" (Adult) and "Delft Blue" (Toddler) for MC, The Yarns of Rhichard Devreize Fynn Worsted 180 yds / 165 m per 85 g skein in "Kristin" (Adult) and "Lake of Bays" (Toddler) for CC.

4.5 mm (US 7) needles for knitting in the round
5.0 mm (US 8) needles for knitting in the round
Or size required to obtain gauge

Tapestry needle

GAUGE
26 sts and 48 rnds = 4" / 10 cm
In stitch pattern with 4.5 mm (US 8) needles.
This gauge appears tighter than typical for a worsted yarn—this is due to the slipped stitch pattern.

SIZES
Baby (Toddler, Child/Adult Small, Adult Medium, Adult Large)
Finished hand circumference: 4.75 (5.5, 6.5, 7.5, 8.5)" / 12 (14, 17, 19, 22) cm

Work Rnds 1–12 0 (1, 1, 2, 2) time(s).
Next work Rnds 1–10 (1–4, 1–10, 1–4, 1–10).

Thumb Insert Rnd
Stitch counts are provided for the Baby size. However, if you omit the thumb, continue to the Hand instructions.

Right Mitten: K1, place next 5 (6, 7, 8, 9) sts on yarn holder/scrap yarn. CO 5 (6, 7, 8, 9) using the backward loop method (see Special Techniques), K to end.

Left Mitten: K to last 5 (6, 7, 8, 9) sts, place next 5 (6, 7, 8, 9) sts on yarn holder/scrap yarn. CO 5 (6, 7, 8, 9) using the backward-loop method, K1.

Purl 1 rnd.

Hand
Starting with Rnd 1 (7, 1, 7, 1), continue working as established until mitten measures approximately 0.5" / 1.5 cm shorter than desired length, ending after Rnd 6 or 12.

Top Decreases
Follow the decrease instructions based on the round you last knit.

Ended after Rnd 6
With CC
Dec Rnd 1: *K1, Sl 2, SSK, K1; rep from * to end of rnd. 25 (30, 35, 40, 45) sts rem.
Next Rnd: *K1, Sl 2, K2; rep from * to end of rnd.
Dec Rnd 2: *K1, Sl 2, SSK; rep from * to end of rnd. 20 (24, 28, 32, 36) sts rem.
Next Rnd: *K1, Sl 2, K1; rep from * to end of rnd.
With MC

INSTRUCTIONS
With 4.5 mm (US 7) needles and MC, CO 26 (32, 38, 44, 50) sts. Join to work in the round, being careful not to twist the sts. Work in K1, P1 ribbing for 10 (10, 12, 14, 14) rnds.
Switch to 5.0 mm (US 8) needles.

Inc Rnd: *K7 (8, 10, 11, 13), M1, K6 (8, 9, 11, 12), M1; rep from * once more. 30 (36, 42, 48, 54) sts.
Next Rnd: Purl.
Next, begin working the wrist of the mitten using the chart.

Dec Rnd 3: *K1, SSK, K1; rep from * to end of rnd. 15 (18, 21, 24, 27) sts rem.

Dec Rnd 4: *P2tog; rep from * to last 1 (0, 1, 0, 1) st(s), P1 (0, 1, 0, 1). 8 (9, 11, 12, 14) sts rem.

Dec Rnd 5: *P2tog; rep from * to last 0 (1, 1, 0, 0) st(s), P (0, 1, 1, 0, 0). 4 (5, 6, 6, 7) sts rem.

Ended after Rnd 12

With CC

Dec Rnd 1: *SSK, K2, Sl 2; rep from * to end of rnd. 25 (30, 35, 40, 45) sts rem.

Next Rnd: *K3, Sl 2; rep from * to end of rnd.

Dec Rnd 2: *SSK, K1, Sl 2; rep from * to end of rnd. 20 (24, 28, 32, 36) sts rem.

Next Rnd: K2, Sl 2; rep from * to end of rnd.

With MC

Dec Rnd 3: *K2, SSK; rep from * to end of rnd. 15 (18, 21, 24, 27) sts rem.

Dec Rnd 4: *P2tog; rep from * to last 1 (0, 1, 0, 1) st(s), P1 (0, 1, 0, 1). 8 (9, 11, 12, 14) sts rem.

Dec Rnd 5: *P2tog; rep from * to last 0 (1, 1, 0, 0) st(s), P (0, 1, 1, 0, 0). 4 (5, 6, 6, 7) sts rem.

Cut yarn, leaving a 6" / 15 cm tail. Thread tail through remaining live sts, pull tightly to close.

Thumb

Place 5 (6, 7, 8, 9) sts from scrap yarn/stitch holder back to size 4.5 mm (US 7) working needle. With MC, P5 (6, 7, 8, 9), PU 1 in the gap, PU and K5 (6, 7, 8, 9) sts from the CO edge, PU 1 in the gap. 12 (14, 16, 18, 20) sts on needle.

Work in St st until thumb measures approximately 1.5 (1.75, 2, 2.25, 2.75)" / 4 (4.5, 5, 6, 7) cm, or until it reaches the length.

Dec Rnd 1: *K2tog; rep from * to end of rnd. 6 (7, 8, 9, 10) sts rem.

Dec Rnd 2: *K2tog; rep from * until 0 (1, 0, 1, 0) st(s) rem, K 0 (1, 0, 1, 0). 3 (3, 4, 5, 5) sts rem.

Cut yarn, leaving a 6" / 15 cm tail. Thread tail through remaining live sts, pull tightly to close.

Finishing

Weave in all ends. For best results, block and lay flat to dry to allow stitch pattern to relax.

CHART

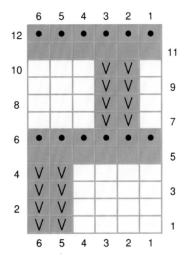

Rows 1–4: With CC, K4, Sl 2; rep to end.

Row 5: With MC, knit.

Row 6: Purl.

Rows 7–10: With CC, K1, Sl 2, K3; rep to end.

Row 11: With MC, knit.

Row 12: Purl.

POLARIS *A snowflake hat*

Made for chilly days, this hat will keep little ears nice and toasty in frigid North Atlantic winds. This hat features simple snowflake and single-stitch colourwork, a Latvian braid, and an optional pompom for extra fun! Instructions include both charted and written instructions and sizes range from newborn to adult to outfit the whole family.

SKILL LEVEL
Intermediate

Skills required: working in the round, stranded colourwork, increasing and decreasing, Latvian braid

MATERIALS
Approximately 105 (117, 130, 144, 160, 176) yds / 96 (107, 119, 132, 146, 161) m worsted-weight yarn; 71 (79, 88, 98, 109, 120) yds /65 (72, 80, 90, 100, 110) MC, 34 (37, 41, 46, 51, 56) yds / 31 (34, 37, 42, 47, 51) m CC. Samples Shown in Sweet Georgia Superwash Worsted "Saffron" (Adult Medium), Biscotte & Cie Merino Worsted "Chardon" (Child), Cascade 220 col. 2433 "Pacific" (Toddler).

4.0 mm (US 6) needles for knitting in the round
5.0 mm (US 8) needles for knitting in the round
5.5 mm (US 9) needles for knitting in the round
Or size required to obtain gauge

Tapestry needle
Optional: Pompom maker
4 (4, 5, 5, 6, 6) stitch markers with one unique marker for BOR

GAUGE
19 sts and 23 rnds = 4" / 10 cm
In colourwork pattern, worked in the round with 5.0 mm (US 8) needles, after blocking

SIZES
Sizes: Baby (Toddler, Child, Adult Small, Adult Medium, Adult Large)
Hat circumference: 13.5 (15, 17, 18.5, 20, 22.75)" / 34 (38, 43, 47, 51, 58) cm
Hat is meant to be worn with 0–2.5" / 0–5 cm of negative ease

INSTRUCTIONS

Using 4.0 mm (US 6) needles, CO 64 (72, 80, 88, 96, 108), place BOR M and join to work in the round. Work in K2, P2 ribbing for 6 (8, 8, 10, 10, 12) rnds.

Change to 5.0 mm (US 8) needles.

Latvian Braid

Rnd 1: *K1 MC, K1 CC; rep from * to end of rnd.
Rnd 2: *P1 MC, bring CC **under** MC strand, P1 CC, bring MC **under** CC strand; rep from * to end of rnd. *The strands will twist together, but they will untwist in the next rnd.*
Rnd 3: * P1 MC, bring CC **over** MC strand, P1 CC, bring MC **over** CC strand; rep from * to end of rnd.

Knit 3 (3, 3, 3, 2, 3) rnds in MC.

Adult Small only: K44, M1, K44, M1 (90 sts).

All sizes

Switch to 5.5 mm (US 9) needles. Work Rnds 1–13 of Chart A (B, A, B, A, B).

Switch to 5.0 mm (US 8) needles and continue working the body of the hat using the following stitch pattern.

Stitch pattern

Adult Small only: K43, K2tog, K43, K2tog. (88 sts). Continue to Rnd 2 below.

All sizes

Rnds 1–4: Knit with MC.

Rnd 5: *K3 MC, K1 CC; rep from * to end of rnd.

Rnds 6–9: Knit with MC.

Rnd 10: *K1 MC, K1 CC, K2 MC; rep from * to end of rnd.

Continue working Rnds 1–10 until hat measures approximately 5.5 (6.5, 7, 7.75, 8.5, 9)" / 14 (17, 18, 20, 22, 23) cm from CO edge, or until hat measures approximately 2" / 5 cm shorter than desired height.

Top Decreases

Adult Small only: K44, M1, K44, M1 (90 sts).

All sizes

Set Up Rnd: *Work in patt for 16 (18, 16, 18, 16, 18) sts, PM; rep from * to end.

Dec Rnd 1: *SSK, work in patt to 2 sts before M, K2tog; rep from * to end.

Dec Rnd 2: Work across the rnd in patt.

Work Rnds 1–2 a total of 3 times. 40 (48, 50, 60, 60, 72) sts rem. Work Rnd 1 4 (5, 4, 5, 4, 5) more times. 8 (8, 10, 10, 12, 12) sts rem. Cut CC, leaving a 6" / 15 cm tail.

Final Dec Rnd: K2tog around. 4 (4, 5, 5, 6, 6) sts rem. Cut MC, leaving a 6" / 15 cm tail. Thread through the live sts rem on the needle, pull tightly to close.

Finishing

Weave in all ends. Blocking is recommended to relax colourwork pattern. Optional: Make pompom and attach to the top of the hat.

CHART A

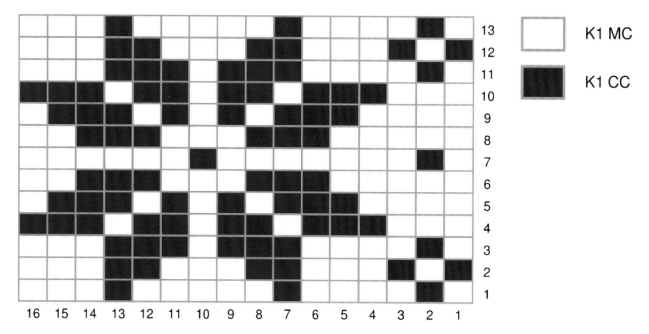

Row 1: K1 MC, K1 CC, K4 MC, K1 CC, K5 MC, K1 CC, K3 MC.

Row 2: K1 CC, K1 MC, K1 CC, K3 MC, K2 CC, K3 MC, K2 CC, K3 MC.

Row 3: K1 MC, K1 CC, K4 MC, K3 CC, K1 MC, K3 CC, K3 MC.

Row 4: K3 MC, K3 CC, K1 MC, K2 CC, K1 MC, K2 CC, K1 MC, K3 CC.

Row 5: K4 MC, K3 CC, K1 MC, K1 CC, K1 MC, K1 CC, K1 MC, K3 CC, K1 MC.

Row 6: K5 MC, K3 CC, K3 MC, K3 CC, K2 MC.

Row 7: K1 MC, K1 CC, K7 MC, K1 CC, K6 MC.

Row 8: K5 MC, K3 CC, K3 MC, K3 CC, K2 MC.

Row 9: K4 MC, K3 CC, K1 MC, K1 CC, K1 MC, K1 CC, K1 MC, K3 CC, K1 MC.

Row 10: K3 MC, K3 CC, K1 MC, K2 CC, K1 MC, K2 CC, K1 MC, K3 CC.

Row 11: K1 MC, K1 CC, K4 MC, K3 CC, K1 MC, K3 CC, K3 MC.

Row 12: K1 CC, K1 MC, K1 CC, K3 MC, K2 CC, K3 MC, K2 CC, K3 MC.

Row 13: K1 MC, K1 CC, K4 MC, K1 CC, K5 MC, K1 CC, K3 MC.

CHART B

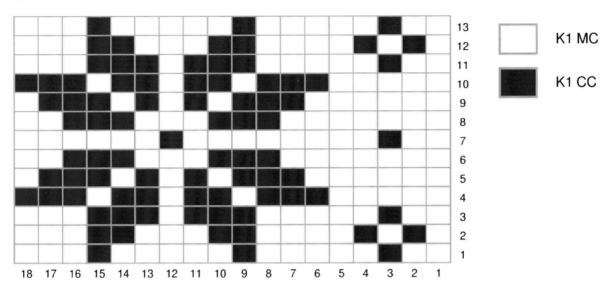

Row 1: K2 MC, K1 CC, K5 MC, K1 CC, K5 MC, K1 CC, K3 MC.

Row 2: K1 MC, K1 CC, K1 MC, K1 CC, K4 MC, K2 CC, K3 MC, K2 CC, K3 MC.

Row 3: K2 MC, K1 CC, K5 MC, K3 CC, K1 MC, K3 CC, K3 MC.

Row 4: K5 MC, K3 CC, K1 MC, K2 CC, K1 MC, K2 CC, K1 MC, K3 CC.

Row 5: K6 MC, K3 CC, K1 MC, K1 CC, K1 MC, K1 CC, K1 MC, K3 CC, K1 MC.

Row 6: K7 MC, K3 CC, K3 MC, K3 CC, K2 MC.

Row 7: K2 MC, K1 CC, K8 MC, K1 CC, K6 MC.

Row 8: K7 MC, K3 CC, K3 MC, K3 CC, K2 MC.

Row 9: K6 MC, K3 CC, K1 MC, K1 CC, K1 MC, K1 CC, K1 MC, K3 CC, K1 MC.

Row 10: K5 MC, K3 CC, K1 MC, K2 CC, K1 MC, K2 CC, K1 MC, K3 CC.

Row 11: K2 MC, K1 CC, K5 MC, K3 CC, K1 MC, K3 CC, K3 MC.

Row 12: K1 MC, K1 CC, K1 MC, K1 CC, K4 MC, K2 CC, K3 MC, K2 CC, K3 MC.

Row 13: K2 MC, K1 CC, K5 MC, K1 CC, K5 MC, K1 CC, K3 MC.

PIXIE A whimsical hat

Pixie is a whimsical bonnet-style hat that pays homage to the mischievous sprites that live in local folklore legends. The hat is knit by holding a DK-weight yarn double with a lace-weight mohair yarn to create a soft and warm fabric with a beautiful halo. It is finished with i-cord ties and edging along the neckline to ensure that the hat stays in place.

SKILL LEVEL
Experienced beginner

Skills required:
knitting flat, seaming, decreasing, i-cord, i-cord bind off, picking up stitches

MATERIALS
Approximately 117 (130, 143, 157) yds / 107 (119, 131, 144) m of DK-weight yarn and lace-weight yarn, to be held double OR 117 (130, 143, 157) yds / 107 (119, 131, 144) m of worsted-weight yarn. Sample shown in Julie Asselin Leizu DK, 260 yds / 238 m per 115 g skein in col. "Avril" and Lichen and Lace Marsh Mohair, 458 yds/420 m per 50 g skein in col. "Sage."

4.0 mm (US 6) needles for knitting flat
4.0 mm (US 6) DPNs
4.5 mm (US 7) needles for knitting flat
Or size required to obtain gauge

Tapestry needle

GAUGE
21 sts and 28 rows = 4" / 10 cm
In stockinette stitch with 4.5 mm (US 7) needles

SIZES
0–6 mo (6–12 mo, Toddler, Child)
To fit head circumference: 15 (17, 19, 21)" / 38 (43, 48, 53) cm

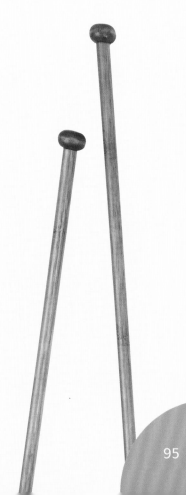

INSTRUCTIONS

With 4.0 mm (US 6) needles and holding one strand each of DK and Mohair yarn, CO 65 (77, 85, 95) sts.

Work in 1x1 ribbing as follows:

Row 1 (RS): *K1, P1; rep from * to the last stitch, K1.
Row 2 (WS): *P1, K1; rep from * to the last stitch, P1.

Repeat Rows 1–2 until the ribbing is 0.75 (0.75, 1, 1)" / 2 (2, 2.5, 2.5) cm, ending after a WS row.

Change to 4.5 mm (US 7) needles. Work in St st until the piece measures 6 (6.75, 7.5, 8.25)" / 15 (17, 19, 21) cm, ending after a WS row.

Shaping

Row 1 (RS): BO 5 sts, K to end.
Row 2 (WS): BO 5 sts, P to end.
10 sts dec.

Work shaping Rows 1–2 a total of 5 (6, 6, 7) times. 15 (17, 25, 25) sts rem.

Row 3: K to last 2 sts, K2tog.
Row 4: P to last 2 sts, P2tog.
2 sts dec.

Work shaping Rows 3–4 until 3 sts remain. K3tog. Cut yarn, leaving a 15" / 38 cm tail. With a tapestry needle, pull the tail through the remaining stitch to fasten, then proceed to seam the two sides using the horizontal seaming method (see Special Techniques) to form the back of the hat.

I-cord Ties and Edging

With 4.0 mm (US6) DPNs, make an i-cord approximately 10.5" / 27 cm in length (see Special Techniques).

Next, pick up sts along the neckline and create the i-cord edge at the same time. Sts are picked up at a rate of 1 stitch for every 2 rows. Place the DPN holding the i-cord you just knit in your right hand. Pick up and K 1 stitch. Slide all 4 sts to the right.

I-cord BO Row: K2, K2tog TBL, pick up and K1 stitch. Slide all 4 sts to the right.

Repeat this row across the neckline edge of the hat. Once you have picked up the last stitch, slide all 4 stitches to the right, K2, K2tog TBL. 3 sts rem.

Continue making an i-cord tie 10.5" / 27 cm in length. Cut yarn, leaving a 6" / 15 cm tail, thread through the 3 stitches on the needle, and pull tightly to close.

Finishing

Weave in all ends. Block if desired.

Special Techniques

Backward-Loop Cast On

Hold yarn and wrap it over your left thumb. Insert the needle in front of the thumb, up and under the yarn. Release the thumb and gently pull yarn to tighten stitch. Repeat for as many stitches as required.

Horizontal Seaming Method

Place the two edges of the pieces together (WS together) so that they are lined up stitch by stitch, one piece on top, one piece below. The seam is worked from right to left. Using a darning needle and working yarn of the same colour, insert your needle under both legs of the first edge stitch on the lower piece from right to left, and pull the yarn through. Next, insert the needle under both legs of the first edge stitch on the upper piece from right to left, and pull the yarn through. Continue working in this manner until you have worked across all stitches.

I-cord

An i-cord is a small, knitted tube that is most often used to create ties for hats and mittens. Using DPNs, CO 3 sts. Slide stitches to the right side of the DPN, K3. Repeat this row until the i-cord is the desired length. At this point, refer to pattern instructions for the next step.

Kitchener Stitch

The kitchener stitch is a method of invisibly grafting together knitting. Your stitches should be on two separate needles/needle points, parallel to each other: one in the front, one in the back. With a tapestry needle and yarn:

* Knit the stitch on the front needle, pull yarn through, leave that stitch on the needle.
* Purl the stitch on the back needle, pull yarn through, leave that stitch on the needle.
* Purl on the front needle, pull yarn through, pull that stitch off the needle.
* Knit on the front needle, pull yarn through, leave that stitch on the needle.

* Knit on the back needle, pull yarn through, pull that stitch off the needle.
* Purl on the back needle, pull yarn through, leave that stitch on the needle.

Repeat the last 4 steps until all stitches have been worked.

Knitted-Lace Bind Off

Work your first two stitches in pattern, insert your left needle into the front of the stitches just worked and K2tog TBL. Work the next stitch in pattern, and like before, insert your left needle into the fronts of both stitches and K2tog TBL. Repeat in this manner until all stitches are worked.

Long-Tail Cast On

Make a slip knot and place the loop on the right needle. You will be working with both the working yarn and the tail. Insert your left thumb and index finger between the two strands of yarn, close the rest of your fingers around the yarn to secure it. Insert the needle under the loop wrapped around your thumb and then going right to left, pick up the yarn wrapped around your index finger. Bring your thumb out of the loop and pull the yarn to tighten the new stitch on the needle. Repeat this for as many stitches as required.

M1L: Make 1 Left

Pick up the bar between the stitches, bringing the needle from front to back, knit the stitch through the back loop.

M1R: Make 1 Right

Pick up the bar between the stitches, bringing the needle from back to front, knit the stitch as usual.

Mattress Stitch

For this seam, you are joining two knit pieces together by grabbing the horizontal bar that runs between the stitches, alternating back and forth. With a tapestry needle and matching yarn, draw the needle under the bar between the two outer stitches of the first row on the first piece and pull the yarn through, leaving a 6" / 15 cm tail. Repeat for the first row for the second piece (without leaving a tail). Go back and forth in this manner, working up the sides of each piece. It will form a zigzag pattern. Every few inches, pull the working thread to close the seam. When completed, cut yarn leaving a 6"/15 cm tail and secure.

Single-Crochet Edge

With the right side facing, insert the crochet hook from front to back into the centre of a knit stitch, take the yarn over the hook, and pull the yarn around the hook back through the fabric. Yarn over, pull the yarn through the loop on the hook. You now have one loop on the hook. Insert the hook into the next knit stitch, yarn over, draw up a loop; yarn over, draw the yarn over through both loops on the hook. Continue across the bind-off edge, working one single crochet stitch in each knit stitch to the corner.

Thrumming

Thrums are pieces of unspun fibre that are knit into the fabric to create a dense, fluffy interior. First, gently pull apart the roving to create pencil-thick ropes. Next, gently draft or pull the fibre so that the fibres are stretched thin. You should be able to see through the piece. Then tear a piece off approximately 6" / 15 cm in length. Create a circle overlapping the ends and then pinch the circle in the middle. Roll the centre between your fingers to slightly felt it (this will help keep the thrum from getting too fuzzy!). The finished result should look like a finished bowtie.

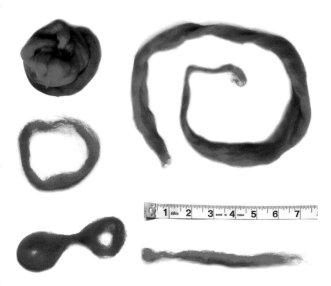

To place the thrum into your knitting, insert your needle into the next stitch, fold the thrum in half so that the felted centre is placed over the needle and knit the stitch with the thrum. The ends of the bow should be facing the inside of your work once knit. On the next row, knit the thrum through the back loop to secure it in place.

Wrap and Turn (W&T)

Knitwise: Knit to point where you need to complete a wrap, and turn. Bring your working yarn to the front, slip the next stitch to your right needle. Turn your work so that the wrong side is facing, bring your working yarn forward again, slip the first stitch to your right needle. The stitch is now wrapped; continue with pattern instructions.

Purlwise: Purl to point where you need to complete a wrap, and turn. Bring your working yarn to the back, slip the next stitch to your right needle. Turn your work so that the right side is facing, bring your working yarn to the back again, and slip the first stitch to your right needle. The stitch is now wrapped; continue with pattern instructions.

Work in Patt(ern)

Continue knitting the piece in the established stitch pattern.

Abbreviations & Glossary

Approx	Approximately
BO	Bind Off
BOR	Beginning of Round
CC	Contrast Colour
CDD	Central Double Decrease Slip 2 stitches Knitwise, K1, pull two slipped sts over the knit stitch
CN	Cable Needle
CO	Cast On
Dec	Decrease(d)
DPN(s)	Double Pointed Needle(s)
Inc	Increase(d)
LN	Left Needle
K	Knit
K2tog	Knit 2 stitches together
K3tog	Knit 3 stitches together
Kwise	Knitwise, as if to knit
M	Marker
M1	Make 1 stitch
M1L	Make 1 Left
M1P	Make 1 purl stitch
M1R	Make 1 Right
MC	Main Colour
P	Purl
P2tog	Purl 2 stitches together
Patt	Pattern
PM	Place Marker
PU	Pick up and knit
Pwise	Purlwise, as if to purl
Rem	Remain(ing)
Rep	Repeat
Rnd(s)	Round(s)

RS	Right Side The side facing outward
Sl	Slip (pwise)
SSK	Slip Slip Knit Slip 1 stitch, slip 1 stitch, knit the two slipped stitches together
St(s)	Stitch(es)
St st	Stockinette stitch
TBL	Through the back loop
W&T	Wrap and Turn
WS	Wrong Side The side facing inward
YO	Yarn Over

Cable Chart Symbols

1/2 RC	Sl 2 sts to CN, hold in back, K1 from LN, K2 from CN.
1/2 LC	Sl 1 st to CN, hold in front, K2 from LN, K1 from CN.
2/1 RPC	Sl 1 st to CN, hold in back, K2 from LN, P1 from CN.
2/1 LPC	Sl 2 sts to CN, hold in front, P1 from LN, K2 from CN
2/2 RC	Sl 2 sts to CN, hold in back, K2 from LN, K2 from CN.
2/2 LC	Sl 2 sts to CN, hold in front, K2 from LN, K2 from CN.
3/3 RC	Sl 3 sts to CN, hold in back, K3 from LN, K2 from CN.
3.3 LC	Sl 3 sts to CN, hold in front, K3 from LN, K2 from CN.
2/1/2 RC	Sl 3 sts to CN, hold in back, K2 from LN, slip the leftmost st from the CN back to the LN, K1 from LN, K2 from CN.
2/1/2 LC	Sl 3 sts to CN, hold in front, K2 from LN, slip the leftmost st from the CN back to the LN, K1 from LN, K2 from CN.

Acknowledgements

Writing this book has been an incredible opportunity and a lot of work, and it never would have happened if not for all the amazing people who have helped along the way.

The first and biggest thank you to my soon-to-be-husband, Matthew, for all his support over the last year and for being just as excited as me about this project. It's been a huge undertaking and it wouldn't have happened without your willingness to take on the extra work to give me the time and space needed. I love you.

To Shirley Scott, you are my guru. Thank you for seeing the possibility in my work and for being a source of guidance through it all. And to Gavin Will and Stephanie Porter at Boulder Books—thanks for taking a chance on me. It has been an absolute pleasure to create this collection and collaborate with you to make this the best it could be.

To my technical editor, Linda Brown, you are nothing short of fantastic. Thank you so much for all the work that went into getting these patterns in shape (and for being so forgiving of my mom-brain).

I also want to say a big thank you to all my test knitters: Kayla, Alison, Georgie, Amy, Debbie, Jenny, Bi, Rhea, Marian, Edny, and Christina. Test knitting is such an important part of pattern writing. Your work and feedback have been absolutely integral to making this book a success.

Finally, a big thank you to all my little models (and their wonderfully co-operative parents) who brought these patterns to life: Sunnie, Jacob, Lily, Jude, Aneurin, Parker, and of course, Philip. I love you all!

About the Author

Knitting and yarn enthusiast turned designer Katie Noseworthy loves to spread the joy of knitting through elegant, contemporary patterns. Designing since 2017, she has successfully published over two dozen patterns and has been featured in collections published by KnitPicks. Katie lives in Newfoundland, with her partner, toddler, and fur-baby, and is rarely found without a project in tow. Occasionally, Katie puts her knitting down to enjoy a good book or a night out.

For any questions about the patterns, please contact the author at knitsforlittleones@gmail.com.